# MORALISM

# Moralism

## A Study of a Vice

Craig Taylor

McGill-Queen's University Press

Montreal & Kingston • Ithaca

© Craig Taylor, 2012

ISBN   978-0-7735-4009-5  (cloth)
ISBN   978-0-7735-4010-1  (paper)

Legal deposit first quarter 2012
Bibliothèque nationale du Québec

Published simultaneously outside North America
by Acumen Publishing Limited

McGill-Queen's University Press acknowledges the financial support of the
Government of Canada through the Canada Book Fund for its activities.

Library and Archives Canada Cataloguing in Publication

Taylor, Craig, 1963-
    Moralism : a study of a vice / Craig Taylor.

Includes bibliographical references and index.
ISBN 978-0-7735-4009-5 (bound).--ISBN 978-0-7735-4010-1 (pbk.)

    1. Ethics. 2. Judgment (Ethics). I. Title.

BJ1031.T39 2011              170              C2011-907509-1

Printed and bound in the UK by MPG Books Group.

# Contents

# Preface

This book is about moralism understood as a kind of vice. I use the term moralism very broadly to cover a class of defects of thought and understanding that apply not only to the practice of making moral judgements but to moral thought and moral theorizing more generally. Inevitably, then, the targets of the philosophical arguments and criticisms I develop in this book are many and varied, and admittedly not everything I have to say about moralism applies equally to all of those targets. So, to give just one example, a moral theory may be moralistic in the negative sense I intend without a particular proponent of that theory being an overt moralizer. All the same, the term moralism does, I think, serve to pick out particular related tendencies of thought as they occur in both specific moral judgements and moral theorizing more generally, and which serve to hinder our understanding of the kind of phenomena that moral judging and theorizing are both responses to. Or so I shall argue.

I cannot provide a detailed account of moralism as I understand it in this short preface; that is the aim of the book as a whole. My more limited aim is twofold: first, to say something about the particular issues and problems related to moralism that I shall examine in distinct chapters; and second, and in the context of introducing these issues and problems, to say something about the conception of moral thought that underlies my characterization of the vice of moralism. In particular in relation to this second aim, I need to acknowledge at the outset that the conception of moral thought I outline in this book challenges certain ideas and assumptions that underlie much of contemporary moral philosophy, at least in the analytic tradition, as will start to become clear below.

To begin, Chapter 1 is in many ways what this preface is not: an extended introduction to the book, including an account of what is distinctive about moralism as opposed to some related ideas and vices. Much of this chapter may seem relatively uncontroversial. What is distinctive and challenging to much moral philosophy, in my account of moralism, only becomes really apparent in Chapter 2, where I argue that certain moral judgements are moralistic in so far as they are not informed by what I shall call certain *primitive* responses to people and situations in which moral judgement seems called for. A particular response I shall focus on is pity as it may accompany our judgement of another's moral transgressions. What, in particular, is distinctive and challenging in my argument is my claim that moral thought and judgement depends on an understanding of other human beings that is itself partly constituted by the kind of primitive responses I discuss.

To get a sense of the challenge, in talking of primitive responses I mean to highlight two aspects of such responses: first, that such responses are *immediate and unthinking* in the sense that they are not mediated by certain prior thoughts we might have about the particular human beings we are responding to. So in the case of pity, for example, it is not as if I first recognize that a person is suffering in a particular way and then respond to them in light of what I recognize. At the same time, however, to say that I respond in such cases immediately and without thinking is not to concede that such responses are merely mindless or instinctive. Rather, and this is their second aspect, such responses are, I shall argue, themselves a *form of recognition* of another's humanity. Thus in the case of pity, for example, I understand something of the nature of human suffering through my pity for another and, through that, an aspect of that other's humanity. The presence of such responses in conjunction with our judgements of another marks the distinction between moral judgements that involve an understanding of those we would judge and judgements that display a lack of such understanding and indicate not serious moral thought or reflection, but mere moralism as I understand it. Of course, all this will require some explaining. However, what follows from my argument and is crucial for my account of moralism is that moral agency is not simply a matter of applying moral concepts, principles or theories in practical deliberations about how one morally ought to act, or ought to have acted, on some occasion. Beyond this, moral agency involves the kind of primitive responsiveness I have highlighted, a responsiveness that is itself an aspect of moral thought.

In Chapter 3 I continue to discuss the kind of primitive responsiveness I have outlined in Chapter 2, but my aim in this chapter is to consider moralism as it is involved in a person's *failure* to trust their own primitive responsiveness on certain occasions and specifically in relation to their experience of certain works of art that may be seen as morally problematic. A central claim of this chapter is that while it is only reasonable that our moral judgements of a given work of art should be based in part on the application of moral ideas and principles to it, what we also need to consider is how our responses to a given work of art may themselves lead us to reflect on, and perhaps to revise, those very moral ideas and principles. Again, my argument draws out how our primitive responses to people and situations that seem to call for moral judgement are an essential aspect of moral thought.

In Chapter 4 I turn from considering moralism as it occurs in specific moral judgements to consider moralism as it occurs in moral theorizing more generally. So I shall argue that certain impartialist moral theories distort our understanding of the varieties of value that contribute to a properly human life, partly because they discount the kind of primitive responsiveness I want to highlight. The argument of this chapter involves, in part, examining certain impartialist responses to the so-called problem of moral demandingness. These impartialist moral theories, I suggest, indicate a distorted conception of moral thought and are moralistic in the sense that they lead to morality overstepping its proper bounds or, as I shall put it, overweening in our lives.

In Chapter 5 I further expand on the ideas I have introduced in Chapter 2 concerning the place of certain primitive responses in moral thought. My specific concern in this chapter is to explore the ways in which certain works of literature may, through provoking the kind of primitive responsiveness I have been concerned with, contribute to enriching moral thought and understanding, and so help us to avoid the dangers of moralism. An important claim defended in this chapter, which challenges more orthodox views in analytic moral philosophy, is that moral thought need not involve, or be seen merely as a means to, making explicit moral judgements. In Chapter 6, however, which is in some ways an extension of Chapter 5, I return specifically to what is involved in making moral judgements and argue that a certain class of moral judgements is essentially personal: that two agents in the same situation may make different moral judgements and both be correct. The argument of this chapter is a direct challenge to the claim, again taken for granted in much contemporary analytic moral philosophy, that moral judgements are always universalizable. Finally, in Chapter 7, which involves the practical application of the conception of moral thought I have developed throughout this book, I examine moralism in public debates, specifically as it features in certain public debates about the actions of political leaders on the world stage.

I am indebted to a number of people and institutions for help in writing this book. A good deal of it was written during a period of study leave from Flinders University and I am grateful to Flinders for this and for a small grant to relieve me of some teaching responsibilities. I am also grateful to the Australian Government and the Australian Academy of Humanities for an International Science Linkages–Humanities and Creative Arts Programme International Fellowship, which enabled me to visit the School of Philosophy at the University of East Anglia (UEA) to work on the book. While at UEA I benefited from insightful comments on early drafts of several chapters by various members of the School of Philosophy and particularly by David Cockburn (now at the University of Wales, Lampeter), Oskari Kuusela and Rupert Read. Drafts of the first six chapters of the book were later presented in an honours and postgraduate seminar at Rhodes University in South Africa and I am grateful to the students attending that seminar and particularly Chris Hartley, Douglas de Jager, Caryn Rippe and Gwendolyn Zorn for their many useful comments. During my time at Rhodes, Ward Jones, Tom Martin, Pedro Tabensky, Francis Williamson, Marius Vermaak, Sam Vice and several other members of the academic staff were extremely generous with their time, and I am grateful for the many insightful comments and other help they provided me with. All these people made me feel most welcome. In Australia I have benefited from comments on various draft chapters by Stephen Buckle, Tony Coady, Garrett Cullity, Raimond Gaita and especially Steven Tudor who commented on the first six chapters and Andrew Gleeson who provided me with extensive comments on the whole manuscript. Alice Crary and Rupert Read, acting as reviewers for Acumen, both provided extensive comments on the completed manuscript and I am very grateful to them. I am also grateful to Molly Murn for proofreading the completed manuscript. Finally, I would like to thank my partner Melinda Graefe for her constant support and encouragement. I cannot hope to adequately characterize that support or encouragement here; suffice it to say, I doubt this book would have been written without it.

Earlier versions of some of the arguments presented in this book have been published previously, although in all cases these arguments have been reworked and expanded. I am grateful to the relevant editors and publishers for permission to use material from the following publications: "Moralism and Morally Accountable Beings", *Journal of Applied Philosophy* **22**(2) (2005), 153–60; "Winch on Moral Dilemma and Moral Modality", *Inquiry* **49**(2) (2006), 148–57; "Art and Moralism", *Philosophy* **84**(3) (2009), 341–53; "Literature, Moral Reflection and Ambiguity", *Philosophy* **86**(1) (2011) 75–93.

Craig Taylor

# ONE

# Moralism and related vices

Moralism, I shall argue, involves a distortion of moral thought, reflection and judgement about both people and events. So understood, moralism can be thought of as a kind of vice related specifically to moral thought and judgement. However, there are, as I shall outline, a number of vices that could be so described. Indeed, it may be argued that moralism is really a kind of blanket term used to signify a range of such vices or human tendencies. Certainly, moralism as a term of moral criticism is commonly used in this sort of way, and I have no desire to quibble with this common usage. But to concede, as I do, that moralism does not admit of a simple or uncontentious definition is not to say that we cannot understand moralism, which is to say, the range of human tendencies that "moralism" seems to cover, somewhat better. This book is partly about examining the complex of human tendencies that may be classified as kinds of moralism, and part of why that is important is to make clear and explicit certain distinct ways in which moral thought and judgement may themselves be distorted.

As will already be clear, in this context I am using the term "vice" very broadly. As I shall argue, moralism sometimes indicates certain kinds of defect in the ways in which we respond to others in our specific moral judgements. So in this sense one can think of moralism as indicating certain defects of character. But beyond this, I shall also argue, moralism can involve thinking about morality, including its place in our lives, in the wrong kind of way, specifically in ways that discount the importance of other (non-moral) values. So moralism involves flaws indicated both by certain tendencies of judgement and action and by tendencies of moral thought more generally. To put the point in Aristotle's terms, moralism, as a defect of both action and thought, encompasses what he called both the moral (character) vices and intellectual vices.

One initial thought we might have about moralism as a vice is that it involves making extreme or excessive moral judgements about people and events that they are involved in, but particularly about particular people and their actions. But while that is a feature of moralism on many occasions, including some that I shall discuss, at other times it may simply be that a moral judgement, say, is inappropriate or uncalled for. Thus in some such cases, as we shall see, we might want to say that a person's moral judgement is unreasonable in the sense that it is wrong to make a judgement in the present case.[1] So morally judging another can be unreasonable even though the judgement is true: even though one is uttering a true proposition. As a first and rough approximation, let us say that to be accused of moralism is to be accused of an excessive or otherwise unreasonable tendency in one's moral thoughts and/or judgements about people or events. So described, moralism involves some kind of vice or failing.

I suggested above one way in which we may initially think of moralism, one according to which moralism involves a certain kind of failing. But one might have another opposing thought according to which moralism is no failing whatsoever. Moralism, we might say, is simply the practice of the moralist, so that to criticize someone for moralism really amounts to the rejection of morality. Of course to claim that someone is a moralist need not be, at least not obviously, to criticize them at all. The moralist *per se* is indeed simply one who makes moral judgements or simply engages in moral thought or reflection about, for example, people, their actions and society generally: a moral philosopher even. Moralism, to the extent that it is a vice, would seem to involve some distortion of the proper activity of the moralist. I am not convinced that the distinction between the moralist and those guilty of moralism can always be so clearly drawn, or that there is not always something faintly suspicious in the *desire*, say, to morally judge others.[2]

Nevertheless, there is, I shall claim, an important distinction to be made between two kinds of people. First, there is the person who seeks to describe, understand and evaluate or judge the morally relevant features of situations, which we might think simply amounts to taking morality seriously. Second, there are those who resort in their public and private moral judgements of others, and perhaps even themselves,[3] to moralism, which we may take to be wrong and sometimes highly offensive. We might distinguish the two types by calling the second not a moralist but a mere moralizer. From here on when I refer to a moralizer as opposed to a moralist I shall mean only this latter type of person: the person guilty of moralism.

## Other moralisms

I have so far considered moralism in only the most ordinary senses of the word. However, moralism also has a number of distinct technical meanings in different fields, so in order to avoid any unnecessary confusion it is worth distinguishing moralism as a vice (as I shall understand it) from these other moralisms: from kinds of moralism that denote specific theoretical movements and ideas.

First and most obviously there is legal moralism: the idea within the philosophy of law that a society's collective moral judgements and values can properly be supported by legal sanction even against acts that do not result in harm to others. While I shall not be concerned to examine legal moralism in this book, certain debates here appear to be somewhat relevant to some aspects of my distinct discussion of moralism. One such debate that I shall mention in a note in Chapter 3 is the famous debate in legal moralism between H. L. A. Hart and Lord Patrick Devlin. This debate focused on a British Government report, the Wolfenden Report, which recommended legalizing homosexual acts between consenting adults in private.[4] Second, more recently moralism has been understood in the field of aesthetics as the view that a moral defect in a work of art is, or at least can be, an aesthetic defect and that a moral merit is, or at least can be, an aesthetic merit. There are a range of positions we might hold here, depending on how extreme the claim is: for example, are moral defects always also aesthetic defects, moral merits always aesthetic merits, or (with either or both merits and defects) only sometimes?[5]

An interesting question is to what extent we might see these moral-isms as connected to moralism as I shall understand it, as a kind of vice. One might, for example, want to argue that the very idea that one might be justified – as Devlin thinks – in using the coercive power of the state simply in support of a society's moral values is itself an example of the vice of moralism. A point of connection between my account of moral-ism and Hart's response to Devlin's legal moralism is Hart's defence of reason or reflection and sympathetic understanding in moral judge-ment. Hart's arguments thus bear on some of what I shall have to say about moralism in the sense I am concerned with. Turning to moralism as a theory in aesthetics, one might think that aesthetic moralism really involves something like the moralization, again in the pejorative sense, of art: that is, the application of moral ideas and concepts to art where they do not apply. I shall consider how aesthetic moralism might lead to moralism in this sense in Chapter 4. While there may be a range of connections between these moralisms and the vice of moralism, they are not the subject of this book, although what I have to say about mor-alism as a vice may – in ways I have just flagged, for example – throw some light on debates in these quite distinct enquiries.

Another kind of moralism worth mentioning, but which I shall not discuss in this book, is moralism as it is used in Christian theology to indicate a kind of theological error or flaw. Thus the Protestant liberal-ism of the late nineteenth and early twentieth centuries was charged with moralism in that its interpretation of Christ's teaching reduced the kingdom of God to the realm of liberal moral values. So, as Alister McGrath notes, Johannes Weiss, in his critique of Protestant liberal-ism, argues that "the idea of the 'kingdom of God' was understood by the liberal Protestants to mean the exercise of the moral life in society, or a supreme ethical ideal" (McGrath 1994: 369). What makes such an interpretation questionable, so the critique went, was the preaching of Jesus about the end of humankind in which the realm of merely human values will be overturned. Interestingly though, the kind of moralism associated with this critique bears some relation to what I shall argue in this book, for a central claim I shall make about moralism is that it involves seeing some things as moral matters when they really are not.

Thus we can say that the account of Protestant liberalism I have just sketched amounts, perhaps, to a reduction of religious values and ideals to moral ones in ways that fundamentally distort religious faith. This general aspect of moralism, which we might say involves an unreasonable moralization of human life and the variety of human values, will become clearer below when I consider a kind of moralism somewhat closer to my own project.

Moralism is also used by a range of other thinkers – although there are not actually many of them – to denote a particular kind of failing in a somewhat similar way to mine in this book. A particular philosopher whose account of moralism as a kind of failing is more directly related to some of what I want to say about moralism is Bernard Williams. Williams's account of moralism has been highly influential and I shall discuss his work on this and related subjects in some detail in Chapter 4. Williams's concern with moralism as he understands it is, in ways I shall explain, tied to his influential criticisms of what he calls the "morality system".[6] Williams's criticism is not of particular moral judgements but of impartialist moral theories as a whole (Kantian and Utilitarian theories being Williams's central target). Such theories are moralistic, Williams claims, in that they involve a failure to recognize that a complete or even adequate human life requires our acceptance of a space in human life outside the scope of morality's demands. Such moralism is manifest not only in the way in which we judge *others* but also in the way in which we judge *ourselves*. Williams's account of moralism fits into my overall account of moralism as a kind of distorted conception of moral thought and judgement: by its overweening, as I call it, in our lives. To say that morality overweens in our life is a *criticism* of impartial morality. When, following Williams, I criticize impartialist conceptions of moral thought and judgement as overweening I mean that they trespass into areas of human life where they have no authority. Thus the issue is not whether moral considerations always trump other non-moral considerations: the kind of impartialist who is my target in Chapter 4 may accept that sometimes moral values are outweighed by other values, but even so, morality may continue to overween in our life to the extent that morality sees its role as *allowing* that on some occasion other values may be weightier. The overweening is thus a matter, as I say, of the *scope* that morality presumes for its own authority: its authority to weigh all values, moral and otherwise. All the same, as will become clear in Chapter 5, however, my account of moralism goes beyond Williams's.

There are a number of other philosophers as well who argue that moralism is a kind of moral failure in something like the way I shall argue in this book. I shall have occasion to refer to some of these philosophers in later chapters, as well as more immediately in the next two sections of this chapter, where I examine the similarities and differences between moralism and a range of other closely related failings.

## Moralism and hypocrisy

To begin, we need to distinguish moralism from hypocrisy. It is often suggested that one thing that is so offensive about moralism is that the moralizer condemns immorality in others while failing to acknowledge their own similar moral failings. This is indeed simple hypocrisy. However, the moralizer need not be a hypocrite; sometimes the moralizer's pronouncements and judgements will be inconsistent with their own conduct, but this need not be so. The politician who, while cheating on his wife, condemns those who fail to respect the covenant of marriage is a hypocrite; however, the Catholic priest who condemns this same infidelity may be a moralizer but he is not a hypocrite (assuming that priest is not, say, sleeping with one of his married parishioners).

One might think that moralism and hypocrisy are alike in that they are both vices related to the making of *moral* judgements. But one can be a hypocrite without advancing a moral judgement at all. Consider a person who publicly proclaims that a particular popular author is a low-minded philistine and not worth reading but secretly reads the said author enthusiastically. Such a person is surely a hypocrite, but their judgement is something like an aesthetic not a moral one. Looked at another way, we might want to say more generally that the hypocrite proclaims the higher (in some moral, aesthetic or other sense) but practises the lower, but this need not be so either. It is easy to imagine the reverse; say, where a man hides a fine aesthetic sensibility because he thinks that such a sensibility will be seen as unfitting for a man to possess. Or think, in a similar connection, of Nietzsche saying: "*The noblest hypocrite.* Never to talk about oneself is a very noble piece of hypocrisy" (Nietzsche [1878] 1996: 181). In these cases there is a conflict between the beliefs or commitments a person presents to others and their actual lives and conduct, a conflict that involves an element of pretence,[7] and that is all that is necessary for the charge of hypocrisy.

Nevertheless, in a wide variety of cases there are illuminating similarities between hypocrisy and moralism. First, what both the moralist and the hypocrite claim may be true in one sense; that is, we might think that infidelity or adultery is a bad thing. This shows how moralism is distinct from, say, racism or sexism; unlike these vices moralism does not necessarily depend narrowly on any faulty beliefs a person may have, including about people in groups different from their own. I shall explore this idea further in Chapter 2. Second, what seems objectionable about both hypocrisy and moralism in the case of moral judgements is that, even granting that the judgements involved are true in the above sense, it is somehow unwarranted that the moralist or hypocrite should actually pronounce these judgements. A common objection to both the hypocrite and moralist, for example, is not that they get things wrong but that they are in no position to criticize or condemn.

Now at this point one might suggest that what is objectionable in the case of moralism is that the person making a negative moral judgement – either in public or in private – about another has no right to make this judgement. Robert Fullinwider (2006) defends an account of moralism along these lines. What the moralist fails to see, one might argue, is that it is only if one has a specific personal relationship to another, or occupies some cultural or institutional role in relation to them, that we are entitled to judge them in certain ways. To give some examples: two people in an intimate relationship have a special right to judge aspects of each other's moral conduct; magistrates and judges have some right to judge our conduct in the public sphere to the extent that our conduct is both immoral and illegal; and professionals have a right sometimes to judge the moral conduct of their peers as it pertains to their professional lives.

However, while there is clearly a moral dimension to judgements dispensed by those within such relationships and occupying such roles, it is limited to what is morally required of a person in order to fulfil those relationships and roles. For example, if a member of the medical profession has a right to judge some aspect of the character of another doctor then that is only because that aspect of character has a bearing on a doctor's ability to perform their professional duties. There is, however, no special right for professionals, judges or even spouses to make more unqualified moral judgements about the relevant parties. The traditional and still most obvious pretender to this role is the priest. Such an example though really just illustrates the point that for secular beings *no one* is in a special position to judge their moral conduct *simpliciter*. But the objection to moralism cannot be that no one, except in the qualified cases just described, ever has a right to morally judge us or at least our actions; that would not be an objection to moralism but to morality as a regulative ideal for any human society.

I do not want to deny that sometimes accusations of moralism may indeed be directed precisely at those who judge others without the right provided by specific personal relationships or roles. My argument is, first, that this does not exhaust the proper scope of moral judgement. There are some matters, such as grave public wrongs, about which any of us has a right to speak and judge both in private and in public. And second, in such cases too, where any of us has a right to make moral judgements, we may be guilty of moralism. So we cannot characterize moralism merely as making moral judgements without a right to do so and in this respect my account of moralism differs sharply with that given by Fullinwider.

## Moralism and self-righteousness

Another vice with close connection – perhaps even closer connection – to moralism is the vice of self-righteousness. We might simply regard self-righteousness as a form of moralism, but there is an important distinction we might make between self-righteousness and moralism as I shall understand it. Moralism involves excessive or otherwise unreasonable negative judgements or assessments of others and perhaps also oneself, whereas self-righteousness involves an agent in making unreasonable positive judgements or assessments about themselves. Self-righteousness may be thought of as an unwarranted sense of one's moral superiority to others. So understood, it is easy to see how self-righteousness and moralism (as I shall understand it) can blend together. In understanding how that might be, two questions are: (i) are the self-righteous necessarily moralizers; and (ii) are moralizers necessarily self-righteous?

To consider the first question, one way in which the self-righteous person's sense of moral superiority may be sustained is by comparing themselves with another about whom their moral judgements and assessments are unreasonably harsh. So the self-righteous person, for example, may also be guilty of moralism in that they make too much of the moral failings of others, which then seems to them to throw their own supposed relative moral merit into sharper relief. In this way moralism may bolster their sense of their moral superiority, but it is not the only source of this sense of superiority. In the most extreme (or purest) kind of case, so secure is the morally self-righteous person's sense of their moral superiority or exceptional excellence of character, so unqualified is their confidence in their own judgements, that they hardly need any such selective and skewed evidence derived from their experience of others in order to sustain this grand but flawed vision of themselves. In such a case it may be that self-righteousness is consistent with an attitude of uncritical, benevolent condescension to others who (one imagines) lack one's moral qualities.

To consider the second point, it is perhaps more plausible to suppose that the moralizer is also always self-righteous to some extent. For it seems to be often in the nature of moralism that the moralizer makes their judgements, as it were, from "on high", that they assume for themselves the moral high ground, a phenomenon I shall consider in some detail in Chapter 7. I have noted that one thing that is so offensive about moralism is that the moralizer condemns, often in the harshest terms, the moral failings of others while failing to acknowledge his own similar moral failings. So we might say that some level of self-righteousness may often be present in those who moralize. To consider possible exceptional cases though, it may be that a moralizer thinks we are *all* (himself included) morally tainted: that we all exist in a state of sin. It is even possible to imagine a kind of moralizer who focuses exclusively on his own moral failings. Thus the account of moralism I develop in this book differs in an important respect from the account of moralism as a vice given by Julia Driver, in that I do not hold, as she does, that moralism is always directed at others. For Driver, moralism involves the "imposition of excessive values or the excessive imposition of values" upon others so that there is, she claims, "a self/other asymmetry in moralism" (Driver 2006: 38).

I have explored the ways in which we might distinguish moralism, hypocrisy and self-righteousness. However, it remains true that they are all in a further sense connected to each other. That is to say, they may all involve a lack of depth or seriousness with respect to moral thought or judgement. In the case of hypocrisy that is plain: the hypocrite is concerned merely with appearances. The case of moralism and self-righteousness is perhaps a little more complicated, for those guilty of these vices are concerned in at least some sense to *be* rather than to just *appear* moral. But what is striking of moralism (and to an extent self-righteousness too) is that a person's concern to be moral is, in ways I shall explore throughout this book, neither serious nor reflective enough to qualify as genuine moral thought or judgement. By genuine moral judgement I mean a judgement that meets what we collectively take to be the standards of thought, discussion and argument as they apply to moral matters quite generally. So by genuine moral judgements, for example, I do not mean true or correct moral judgements. There can be moral disagreements between people each of whom is making a genuine moral judgement, and the same holds for disagreements over other kinds of judgement as well. To further explain this point, compare the case of art criticism. Two people can have a disagreement about whether, say, a painting is a great work of art or not and both can be making genuine aesthetic judgements. But as opposed to this there will be judgements that fall short of the standards of thought, discussion and argument as they apply in art criticism. So if there is a disagreement over the aesthetic merit of Jackson Pollock's *Blue Poles* and someone offers the judgement "My ten-year-old son could do that", we are entitled to say that is not a genuine aesthetic judgement in the sense of "genuine" that concerns me. Of course, to consider a different point, in saying that the moralizer's judgement is not sufficiently serious, one has to acknowledge the fact that the moralizer takes their own moral thoughts and judgements very seriously; but moral thought and judgement requires much more than that. Understanding better *what* more is required here, or more precisely what genuine moral thought and judgement requires *of us*, is a central aim of this book.

## Moralizing about moralism

I have been trying to get clear, or clearer, about the nature of a kind of failing to which we may succumb in making moral judgements and in moral thought more generally. What I shall go on to consider in the next chapter is an example where people do succumb to this failing, and in the chapter after that I shall turn directly to examine the character of some of those who moralize. Now this might seem to invite the following kind of objection to the project of this book: in so far as I want to accuse others of moralism, simply in making this accusation could I not myself be likewise guilty of moralism? That is indeed an important question, for if, in my discussion of what is wrong with moralism, I succeed in doing nothing more than point a moral finger at those who point a moral finger at others, I shall have achieved nothing. But while that question serves as a kind of warning to any such project as this, it does not in itself show that any such project is wrong-headed. Here it is important to say something more about the nature of this project.

First, while I obviously cannot avoid advancing some moral judgements, including about certain people, the *point* of this book is not to judge, let alone condemn anyone. This book is an examination of the nature of moral judgements and of one broad kind of way in which they may be distorted: distorted in a way that suggests (or ways that suggest) a kind of failing. In doing this I shall need to refer to moral debates in which moralism, I contend, plays a part, and a particular sticking point may be my discussion of issues that remain deeply morally contentious. In asking the reader to consider whether, in morally contentious cases, a given person's moral judgement of people or events really involves moralism, I recognize that people may form somewhat different moral views about the cases themselves. But my interest in these cases and what I think we might learn from them does not depend on people drawing *all* the same conclusions about them. Moreover, focusing exclusively on the moral judgements we might be inclined to make *specifically about* such morally contentious issues – I mean what we take to be the "rights" and "wrongs" of the particular case – really serves to obscure the point of these cases as I use them.

The point may be clearer if I turn briefly to one of the cases I shall look at. I suggest in Chapter 3 that a recent debate over certain photographs of naked adolescents by the Australian artist Bill Henson was distorted by moralism; in particular, I shall claim that many of those who condemned Henson are arguably guilty of moralism. Now, if one thinks that Henson's photographs are morally problematic, one might simply want to say these people were right to condemn Henson, so there was no moralism. But note that we can accept that at least some of what was said in criticism of these images was true (or that there was some truth in what was said) but think also that it was somehow unreasonable or excessive to make the specific moral judgements that some people made. As I have already noted, it may be that what the moralizer says is true, but that it is somehow unreasonable to make this judgement in the present case. Thus, in the furore over Henson, one might think that it is unreasonable (moralistic) to proclaim one's moral concerns publicly and often in a context in which the families of the children involved are subject to intense and sometimes hostile media scrutiny. Further, and even worse, it is one thing to have moral concerns about Henson's photographs and another to compare Henson and the parents of his child models to pornographers, and that is what some people did.[8]

One sure way to miss the point I want to make is to proceed like this: "I think these photographs by Henson are morally objectionable; Taylor is just wrong". For the issue here is not about whether I am right or wrong about Henson. In fact, *about the Henson case* there is nothing, in one sense, that I am aiming to be right about; I concede that one might reasonably morally object to Henson's images of naked adolescents. I myself do not think they are morally objectionable, but to focus on that judgement is just to muddy the waters; my own specific judgement about this particular case is not central to the point I want to make. I said I do not find Henson's photographs morally objectionable, but my point about moralism does not depend on you agreeing with *that*. I am concerned only with the manner in which the debate about Henson was conducted and the manner in which people judged him. I am not accusing anyone who finds Henson's images morally objectionable of anything. I am interested in using this example only to draw out one way in which moral thought and judgement, and then debate, may be distorted by moralism. Of course, there is another kind of disagreement we might have: you might simply disagree that the debate over Henson was distorted by moralism. But that is a separate issue; two people might disagree about whether Henson's photographs are morally objectionable but agree that the debate was distorted by moralism.

To put the point above slightly differently, while I shall consider cases that involve calls for the censorship of art and legal sanctions to be imposed on artists and galleries, such as the case above, I am not, in examining moralism in connection to such claims, defending the rights of artists or any particular theory of freedom of expression. That would be to make and to defend specific moral judgements on the basis, say, of specific moral principles and theories. But this book is not a work in what is commonly called theoretical normative ethics. I neither offer nor defend a theory of ethics; in fact, as will become clear, I am sceptical about the capacity of ethical theories to capture or make sense of moral reflection and judgement in a variety of cases. It would be better to understand the book as a work in part of metaethics: a work concerning in part the nature and status or moral judgements *per se*, but one with implications for the practice of moral reflecting on, and judging, people and events. So, crudely, the book is part metaethics, part applied ethics. That, I admit, is *very* crude, but it does serve to underline the point that I shall not be taking sides to defend any theory of ethics, any theory that might then return some substantive claim about, say, the moral limits of censorship. You might think I have rather laboured the above points, but there is a reason for taking some time here. Many people, including perhaps many who take the time to read books of moral philosophy, take morality pretty seriously. While there is plenty of moral hypocrisy in this world it remains true that many people want really to be, and not just to appear, moral. Our confidence that we are living a moral life is tied very closely to our sense of ourselves, to our sense of our own identity. For this reason the faintest suggestion that we might be guilty of moralism may strike us as a very personal attack. I more or less expect, then, a kind of "touchiness" in response to some of what I shall argue and especially with respect to my treatment of certain morally contentious issues. So it is important to emphasize that I am not suggesting that if, with respect to some morally contentious issue, a given person has moral objections not shared by others then they must be guilty of moralism. To such people and about such issues I say this: with moralism I am attempting to describe a common human vice, not passing a judgement on the particular judgements of others, and it is up to you to determine whether or not there are traces of moralism, as I have described it, in your life.

But our possible touchiness, as I put it above, is a problem. Part of the difficulty of moralism is that while morality may have, as I have suggested, personal importance in our lives, it is obviously not enough for living a moral life that *morality is personally important to us*, for, thought of in one way, that can easily lead to, or be corrupted into, the wrong kind of interest in morality: an interest in being thought of or treated in a certain way (an interest in others accepting one's good character) as opposed, say, to an interest in helping others in need or in acting justly (the sorts of things that morality is really about). The hazard of moralism is that moral seriousness is corrupted into a demand that others relate to oneself and one's judgements in a certain way. Part of the problem with moralism is, and this will be crucial in what follows, that it may be difficult to see how one might guard against *this* hazard by one more exercise of moral judgement. Here we need a somewhat richer conception of moral thought and reflection.

To explain the above thought, both the real danger with a work like this of simply descending into the morally suspect judging of others (the very thing I want to warn against) and the suspicion that that is all I am (or can be) doing can be explained by the prevalence of an inadequate account of what moral thought and judgement really involves. According to this conception, moral thought is most fundamentally about (moral thought is a means to) making moral judgements, where moral judgement is understood roughly to involve the application of moral concepts, principles and theories to actions, people and events. The result of moral thought on this conception is that we should be able to assert a particular proposition, say, "It is wrong to commit adultery", or issue an imperative such as "You ought not to commit adultery". Against this conception I shall suggest that moral thought is not simply about making moral judgements in this sense.[9] Beyond this conception, moral thought may involve, for example, a kind of knowing *how* to respond to a particular situation as opposed to knowing *that* something is the case, as in an assertion such as "It is wrong to commit adultery".

In exploring the tendency *in* our moral thought and judgements to moralism, I shall consider the ways in which morality involves something more than making moral judgements, as I have just characterized it. First, as I have already flagged, I shall consider how specific judgements we make may be faulty – excessive, harsh, inappropriate or otherwise unreasonable – even though what we say is true, in a perfectly ordinary (or minimal) sense. So, in a sense it may be perfectly correct to say "He was wrong to commit adultery". Nevertheless, it may be, for example, that the terms in which that judgement is expressed may be excessively harsh, or that the occasion on which it is expressed is inappropriate in ways that invite the charge of moralism. Second, I shall consider how there will also be occasions when moral thought need not issue in specific moral judgements at all: when such thought is expressed in and constituted by certain other capacities of moral response. Thus it may be that moral thought issues not in a judgement but simply in a certain emotional response, for example to show pity or sympathy for another.

This book may indeed be considered an exercise in moral thought in the wider sense just characterized, and part of my focus will be on looking at modes of moral thought that do not involve making moral judgements in the narrower sense I have indicated: that is, applying moral concepts, principles or theories to actions, people and events. A particular concern here will be the role of art, and especially literature, as possible modes of moral thought. To be clear, I am not suggesting that such an exercise in moral thought will have no practical consequences; one hope is that on the basis of such thought one will be more alert to the dangers of moralism in the practice of moral judging. Further, the reason we might say that such thought counts as moral thought is precisely that it involves us *responding* in morally thoughtful and significant ways to certain situations that confront us. But, and this is crucial, in responding in such ways we need not be doing so on the basis of some moral judgement we have made. Others may judge us to have acted justly or humanely; but as it is *for us*, we may simply act in ways that are immediate and, in a sense I shall describe, unthinking.

A detailed explanation of what I mean by an immediate and unthinking response must wait until the next and subsequent chapters; however, one can gain a sense of what I have in mind by considering certain everyday examples. It is common for people's moral sensibility to show itself in their acting in ways that are not themselves the product of prior and specific thought or deliberation about how one ought to act in some case. Consider, for example, walking down a busy street talking with someone, a friend, say, and their reaching out a hand to restrain you from walking into traffic. In an unbroken conversation – for it is easy to imagine the conversation continuing throughout this whole event – that restraint is an immediate response, a response that is not itself the product of this person's specific moral thoughts or deliberation. Such a response is an example of the kind of immediate and unthinking responses I mentioned above. A feature of such responses is that, while they are not really the result of specific moral thoughts and reflection, they are not, all the same, thoughtless. Such responses display an attentiveness to others, or awareness and concern for others, which we might describe as a kind of engagement with those around us. Further, the moral significance of such responsiveness becomes clear if we consider that it is a kind of engagement that cannot, in fact, always be relied on, for it is easy enough to find people who lack it. To act in such a way is both immediate and morally thoughtful; it displays a kind of presence of mind with respect to others.

To be attentive to other human beings in the way I have just described is an important dimension of the moral life. Yet such attentiveness is not, I shall argue, a matter of becoming good at making correct moral judgements. What it takes is something like what I called above "presence of mind": something that involves one in acting in ways that require more than the kind of thinking that leads to the assertion of propositions or imperative statements, such as "I ought to help". An aspect of moral thought, in the broad sense that interests me, involves being present to and for others in something like the way this example illustrates. And one part of what I shall argue in this book is that, while certain literature both expresses and may encourage in the reader this kind of engagement with other human beings, such literature is barely, if at all, concerned with determining correct moral judgements. So literature, or at least one kind of literature, is very much concerned with our moral engagement with, and understanding of, other human beings and their lives in ways that extend beyond the making of specific judgements about how one ought to act.

TWO

# *The Scarlet Letter*:
# "a tale of human frailty and sorrow"

I suggested in the previous chapter that moral thought may be expressed in responses that are immediate and unthinking: in responses that are not mediated by moral judgement. In particular, I suggested there will be cases in which moral thought does not issue in moral judgement at all but rather in immediate emotional responses such as pity or sympathy. In this chapter I shall begin to explain what I mean by that, and I will do so by focusing first on a situation where it *is* appropriate actually to make a moral judgement. My concern will be to show, in this case, what may be lacking in our moral thought beyond our judgement of another, and specifically how a person may be guilty of moralism even though their moral judgements are, in a sense, correct, which is to say even though they correctly apply certain moral concepts and principles to the person they are judging. As I indicated in the previous chapter, moral thought involves more than the application of moral concepts, principles and theories to actions, people and events. In this chapter I shall examine a particular example of moralism, an example of one way in which moral thought is distorted by moralism and, in so doing, begin to outline and explain the kind of wider conception of moral thought that I alluded to in the previous chapter.

A central thought about judgements that we might label as moralistic is, as I have noted, not that such judgements are false but that they are flawed in other ways. In this chapter I shall consider one such way in which such moral judgements are flawed. The judgements I shall discuss here are moralistic not because they are false or inaccurate but because they involve a failure to recognize, in ways I shall outline, the humanity of the person who is being judged. The importance of this kind of recognition and the thought or reflection it involves suggest a dimension to moral thought that extends beyond merely making moral judgements. Or so I shall argue. By focusing on one extreme example of moralism I hope to show how, where a person morally judges another, the *manner* in which they judge them – involving the responses that accompany or fail to accompany their judgement – may indicate a failure to recognize the other's humanity.

## Moral judgement and pity

The example of moralism I shall focus on comes from literature, specifically from Nathaniel Hawthorne's novella *The Scarlet Letter* ([1850] 1960).[1] While moralism does not, I have already conceded, admit of any simple or easy definition, few would quibble with the claim that, at least *prima facie*, this story presents a striking example of moralism. Hawthorne's story tells of Hester Prynne, recently arrived in advance of her husband at the Puritan colony of Boston. In her husband's absence Hester commits adultery and is sentenced to the following punishment: to stand at the pillory in front of the whole community with her infant daughter Pearl – the product of her sinful union – wearing a scarlet letter "A" on her breast and thenceforth to wear this emblem for the remainder of her days. Hester's ordeal at the pillory and the way she is treated by her community thereafter illustrate, I shall suggest, the worst excesses of the vice of moralism. Hester's punishment is nothing less than to be cast out of the community altogether, becoming merely "the general symbol at which the preacher and moralist might point" (*ibid.*: 79):

> Every gesture, every word, and even the silence of those with whom she came in contact, implied ... that she was banished ... The poor ... whom she sought out to be the objects of her bounty, often reviled the hand that was stretched forth to succor

> them. Dames of elevated rank, likewise ... were accustomed to
> distil drops of bitterness into her heart ... Clergyman paused
> in the street to address words of exhortation, that brought a
> crowd ... If she entered a church, trusting to share the Sabbath
> smile of the Universal Father, it was often her mishap to find
> herself the text of the discourse.                   (*Ibid.*: 84–5)

But Hester is not alone in her sin, and *The Scarlet Letter* is also the story
of Arthur Dimmesdale: Hester's minister – and Pearl's father. What we
make of Dimmesdale, I suggest, goes to the heart of moralism.

Unlike Hester's sin, Dimmesdale's sin remains a secret. Lacking the
courage to confess his sin, he compounds it with the most appalling
hypocrisy. Eloquently addressing his adoring congregation, he conceals
from them his transgression of one of the most sacred commandments
of his faith. But Dimmesdale is not a shameless hypocrite: he judges
himself more harshly even than his own congregation would. The tragedy of Dimmesdale is that while he is consumed with remorse, cowardice continually draws him back just as he is about to openly admit
his guilt. As Hawthorne says, although he had stood in the pulpit and
declared himself the "worst of sinners" more than a hundred times, he:

> well knew – subtle, but remorseful hypocrite that he was! – the
> light in which his vague confession would be viewed ... He had
> spoken the very truth, and transformed it into the veriest false-
> hood. And yet, by the constitution of his nature, he loved the
> truth, and loathed the lie, as few men ever did. Therefore, above
> all things else, he loathed his miserable self!        (*Ibid.*: 143)

Dimmesdale is tortured by guilt but lacks the strength to publicly confess his sin, so every good and noble impulse he has is corrupted to the
point where his character teeters on the point of total ruin. So in his
anguish Dimmesdale even returns, in the dead of night, to the pillory
where Hester suffered her first ordeal: "No eye could see him ... Why,
then, had he come hither? Was it but the mockery of penitence? A
mockery, indeed, but in which his soul trifled with itself! A mockery
at which angels blushed and wept, while fiends rejoiced, with jeering
laughter!" (*ibid.*: 146–7).

Shocking hypocrite that Dimmesdale is, the point I want to make about him is not that he is also guilty of moralism; as I understand moralism, he is not guilty of that. Rather, my point is that this most miserable man presents a great temptation *to* moralism. That is to say, when we think of Dimmesdale it is all too easy for us to succumb to moralism; it is all too easy for us to hold Dimmesdale up merely as a kind of "general symbol at which the preacher and moralist might point". My claim is that to see Dimmesdale, as the Puritans of Boston see Hester, merely as a token of a type of moral failure would be to miss the central insight of Hawthorne's tale. For, as *The Scarlet Letter* makes plain, nothing is so indicative of moralism than to see in the ruin of a person's life nothing but a moral example and lesson. What is missing from such a portrait of Dimmesdale is, as the angels that Hawthorne refers to show us, pity.

To expand on the above point, consider again the case of Hester. What is most shocking about *The Scarlet Letter* is the townsfolk's almost total lack of pity for her. To be more precise, what is shocking is not just their lack of pity for the humiliation and abuse Hester frequently suffers or for her ostracism more generally, but also their lack of pity for Hester's *guilty* suffering. One thing the townsfolk fail to see or acknowledge is that Hester understands and suffers the burden of her guilt. To illustrate this point, the women of the town are scandalized that Hester should have embroidered her scarlet letter with her own beautiful needlework, seeing in this nothing but contempt for their judgement upon her. Only one among them, the youngest, has the insight to see that in truth "Not a stitch in that embroidered letter, but she has felt it in her heart" (*ibid.*: 56). To her husband Hester says, without any hint of insincerity or self-deception, "I have greatly wronged thee" (*ibid.*: 75).

Of course, almost anyone reading *The Scarlet Letter* today will agree that there is *something* wrong, indeed morally objectionable, about the way in which the Puritans treat Hester. The more interesting question is: *what* exactly goes wrong here? In order to answer that question we need to attend, I shall argue, not to Hester's treatment at the hands of the Puritans, but to our own possible response to Dimmesdale. I said above that Dimmesdale was a great temptation to moralism and I think that it is part of Hawthorne's aim that we shall feel thus tempted. In order to show us the nature of moralism, Hawthorne is inviting us, I think, to attend to our own possible responses to Dimmesdale. My point is to suggest that it is not any (mistaken) judgement of the facts that is at issue here, but an aspect of our responsiveness, or rather lack of responsiveness, to others: that we may respond without pity, for example. To expand on that thought, one way – as I shall argue, the wrong way – to characterize what goes wrong with the Puritans is to say that they simply make the wrong judgement, say because their normative perspective is somehow distorted. What is wrong with that way of characterizing this case is that it implies that there is a (correct) perspective from which the problem of moralism just disappears; if the Puritans had seen things correctly they would not have judged Hester as they did and there would be no problem with moralism. If it was just a matter of seeing the moral features of this situation correctly then we might think that in so far as we lack the distorted moral perspective of the Puritans we are less susceptible to moralism. But we are not; what the Puritans lack in relation to their judgement of Hester we may lack in our judgement of Dimmesdale. Moralism is not, I want now to argue, a matter of not seeing the moral facts correctly but most fundamentally of lacking a certain responsiveness to another,[2] the kind of responsiveness that is involved in viewing another, in a case like this, with pity.[3]

## Response as a form of recognition

I am not though suggesting that moralism about Dimmesdale is simply a certain lack of pity for him. Rather, I am suggesting that a lack of pity in this case may involve a lack of understanding of another, a lack that is itself a kind of failure of moral thought or perception. One way to put the point is to say that moralism involves a lack of fellow feeling and, in this, a failure to fully recognize or acknowledge the humanity of the particular person being judged. Much more generally, I contend that pity is *a form of recognition of another's suffering*. The point I want to make here is both radical and, in a way, subtle, and it will take some explaining so as to make it clear and to see what it suggests about the nature of moral thought. To begin, consider what Peter Winch has said in a similar connection:

"Poor man! How he will suffer." Those of course are the accents of pity. It is in the context of relationships involving such expressions (amongst numberless others of course) that we understand what suffering is. That does not mean that it is impossible for anyone to know that someone else is suffering without pitying him; but it does mean that one cannot (unless a very special context is supplied) ask why the fact that someone is suffering should be a reason for pitying him.

(Winch 1987: 153)[4]

Winch's point is that pity is not simply evidence that we recognize how another may suffer: recognize this, as we might say, *quite independently of our response*. For what suffering means, or is, is given to us through responses such as pity. This does not mean, again as Winch makes plain, that if one does not pity someone in a situation like this then one necessarily fails to recognize their suffering; there are plenty of reasons why pity might not be forthcoming – perhaps we are just too distracted, tired or world weary to respond. The point is though that there is no question, in the usual kind of case, that where another suffers they are an appropriate object of pity, as there would be if one were inclined to ask why the fact they suffered was any reason to pity them. The point might become clearer if we consider an unusual kind of case, for example, where a person's suffering serves some symbolic purpose for them, as when suffering is endured as part of some initiation process. Suffering in that kind of case may lead us to ask whether it is appropriate to pity that person. But to return to the usual case, say where a person has lost a loved one, there is no scope for the question "Why is this any reason for pitying them?" For there is no reason we might give in answer to it. In this more usual case, to recognize the suffering of another human being just is to recognize them as an appropriate object of pity.

It may be argued that some people recognize another as suffering but fail to recognize them as an appropriate object of pity: the sociopath would be an extreme example. But there is, I think, a real question whether the sociopath really understands what human suffering is, or at least a question whether they understand it in the full or substantial sense that the rest of us do. There is, I suggest, a kind of radical disconnect in our relations with the sociopath so that in this dimension of human life – to do with human suffering, but perhaps to do with more besides – there appears to be nothing we might say or do to communicate to him, to impress on him, the meaning of something so basic that it is more or less taken for granted in our commerce with the rest of humanity. A less extreme example would be a person who recognizes that all people suffer but does not see the suffering of at least some people as any reason for pitying them. The racist or slave-owner may be an example here. But a natural reason the slave-owner will give, not for his lack of pity but for his not finding pity appropriate, will be precisely that his slaves do not suffer as his fellow whites do. Once again there is failure of the slave-owner to recognize a dimension in the experience of his slaves: not a failure, to be sure, that is as extreme or disordered as the sociopath's failure, but perhaps because it is not really a disorder the failure is not in the end so insurmountable. As Stanley Cavell has suggested, thinking of the attitude of the slave-owners of the American South to their slaves, "He means, and can mean, nothing definite … He means, indefinitely, that they are not *purely* human", so that:

> if … the justification for [this form of slavery] was pushed to its final ground – that the slave is not a full human being – then that human misery represented an awful form of human progress; for that ground cannot in the long run be maintained. (Cavell 1979: 376–7)[5]

I have been discussing pity, but there are, again as Winch notes, other related responses, responses that are likewise forms of recognition of the suffering of another. One other such response that I have discussed in detail elsewhere is sympathy, which I take to be the phenomenon of being moved to help another who is suffering (Taylor 2002).[6] Sympathy, pity and other related responses to another's suffering can, I suggest, be helpfully thought of as *primitive* in two distinct although connected ways. First, such responses are *immediate and unthinking* in the sense that they need not themselves be mediated by prior thoughts or reflections on the experience of another; it is not as if we first recognize all that is involved in another person suffering and then decide to pity them; rather, our understanding is founded on responses that are quite immediate. Second, which follows from the first sense, such responses are *explanatorily basic*, by which I mean that our responses are internal to our conception of another's suffering, rather than it being the case that our (supposedly independent) conception of another's suffering explains our response. Hence we can say that our responses are, in fact, partially constitutive of our understanding of what suffering is.

## Guilty suffering

I have been concerned to outline how certain responses to another's suffering are partially constitutive of our understanding of what suffering is. But it is important to note further that the suffering at issue is *human* suffering, and we need to remember that for a human being suffering involves more than physical pain and hardship. This brings me back to *The Scarlet Letter*. Among the many ways in which a human being may suffer is the recognition of the wrong they have done to another. Socrates famously argued that it was better to suffer evil than to do it. If that is right then we might take it to show how terrible it may be for a human being to find themselves an evildoer. This is not to say every evildoer or wrongdoer will suffer in the way I am suggesting, but merely to point out that it is part of what it is to be human – part of what it is to suffer in the ways that human beings do – that we may suffer in our guilt: that there is such a thing as guilty suffering. Nor, again, is this to say that if we do not pity someone then we necessarily fail to recognize how they suffer. Again, there are many reasons why pity might not be forthcoming, and in such complex cases of suffering one important reason may be that our most immediate response to the way another person is responding to some moral calamity is one of doubt. Hence we might wonder about the nature of their suffering, about whether it really involves recognizing the moral significance of what they have done, as may be the case where we suspect a person suffers not so much in recognition of their guilt but just in the loss of their good name.[7] However, a failure to recognize another as even an appropriate object of this kind of pity is another matter; this does involve a failure to recognize that person's humanity.

This last kind of failure, moreover, does seem to describe the Puritans of Boston. For them, Hester ceases to be an individual human being in an important sense and becomes "the figure, the body, the reality of sin" (Hawthorne [1850] 1960: 79). Specifically, Hester's identity as a morally accountable being even *capable* of acknowledging guilt and expressing remorse does not figure in their judgement of her. Hence Hester becomes "the fallen woman", no more a real person than the rake in Hogarth's series of paintings (and subsequent engravings) *A Rake's Progress*. And my point is, as I say, that there is something deeply morally offensive in reducing other human beings to such caricatures. At the very least, we owe it to those we would judge to view their actions as the actions of real morally accountable beings.[8] But what follows from this is that what serious moral thought demands of us, beyond a judgement of wrongdoing, is that we respond in certain appropriate ways to the wrongdoer. So, it makes all the difference to the way we view – I mean *morally* view – Hester (or even Dimmesdale) that we recognize, through our pity, that they suffer in the way that they do: that they suffer the pangs of remorse.

I have focused on the lack of pity the townsfolk had for Hester. But pity is, as I have noted, just one response through which we may (as the moralizer does not) acknowledge the humanity of those we would judge. One other comparable moral response to a person clearly guilty of wrongdoing may be a moral form of mercy, to refrain from condemning them.[9] Mercy here involves recognizing what the moralist fails to recognize: that a person's wrongdoing is not all that (morally) matters; that our response to them should not be determined merely by this. In the case of Hester, such mercy would involve recognizing that she suffers as one who understands the full significance of her wrongdoing and that, given this, it is inappropriate, even perverse, to continue to dwell, or expect Hester to dwell, on this wrongdoing. However, I would just note that there is a crucial difference in the scope of pity and mercy, as the case of poor Dimmesdale makes clear. To explain: unlike the case of pity, our mercy for a wrongdoer depends, first, on their sin being known to us, and then on our ability to actually ameliorate their condition in some way (e.g. by not condemning them). But part of what makes us pity Dimmesdale is that he places himself beyond the possibility of mercy when there is, in his case, every prospect of mercy (and even forgiveness) were he only to find the courage to admit that he is Pearl's father. As Hawthorne says of Dimmesdale, "All that guilty sorrow, hidden from the world, whose great heart would have pitied and forgiven" (*ibid.*: 138).[10]

I have suggested that moral thought involves more than simply making a moral judgement about someone: in the case of Dimmesdale or Hester, something beyond our negative moral judgements of another. However, it might be argued, as I noted above, that what the present example really shows is simply that the Puritan townsfolk of Boston make the *wrong* moral judgement: the townsfolk judge Hester too severely, in fact out of all proportion to the severity of her sin. Proportionality is itself, then, part of judging rightly. I agree that what might also strike us about the townsfolk's response to Hester is their exaggeration of Hester's wrongdoing. (There are much worse sins than Hester's, not least of which is, of course, Dimmesdale's hypocrisy.) However, such exaggeration indicates not so much a wrong, in the sense of disproportionate, moral judgement, as simple caricature. The townsfolk's exaggeration of Hester's wrongdoing expresses their caricature of Hester as "the fallen woman". We might even say that such exaggeration is one way in which the moralizer may avoid recognizing a wrongdoer as a real, morally accountable, human being.

The Puritans of Boston do judge Hester too severely. But moralism does not involve a simple lack of proportion. That is part of why I have invited the reader to consider our possible moralism in our responses to Dimmesdale. In many ways Dimmesdale's moral failure is, of course, much more serious than Hester's (and not, I mean, just because he is a minister). And it is partly for that reason that he is more pitiable than Hester. The severity of our judgement of Dimmesdale does not stand against, but rather with, our pity for him; pitying Dimmesdale as we do is not being proportionate, it is not making any sort of balanced judgement with respect to him. Responding to Dimmesdale in ways that express our moral understanding of this case does not reduce to responding with the right degree of severity. On the contrary, I have argued that what expresses our understanding is nothing other than our response to Dimmesdale in all its complexity, not just our judgement on him but the pity that may inform that judgement.

What I am suggesting is that our pity, in a case like this, is contemporaneous with our moral judgement: that it is false to suppose that what must come first is our moral judgement of Dimmesdale and that our pity for Dimmesdale follows from that. For what accompanies and informs our moral judgement is pity, mercy or related responses, the kinds of responses through which we understand what such suffering is. Now this is not to deny that there may be occasions when we might wonder whether or not it is appropriate to pity someone in some way: that this is never open to debate.[11] In a given case it is possible, as I have noted, to doubt that a person really does suffer the pangs of remorse: that they suffer in *this* way. But what I am suggesting is that such doubts depend on a background of primitive responsiveness to other human beings in which such doubts do not arise, and that helps to constitute our sense of what it is to be a human being, which is to say a being that is at least capable of suffering the pangs of remorse. It is possible, even in Dimmesdale's case, to doubt that he really does suffer the pangs of remorse, but it is a different matter to ask why the moral ruin of his life, so wonderfully captured by his night vigil at the pillory, is, in a more general way, any reason to pity him. What may make angels weep here is perhaps simply what Dimmesdale has become, and to recognize Dimmesdale as an appropriate object of this more general kind of pity is to recognize his humanity: that he remains a morally accountable being.

Thus, on my understanding of the relevant responses, it makes sense to talk about a form of moral thought that involves something more than simply making moral judgements. Make any correct moral judgement you like about Dimmesdale (that he is a terrible hypocrite, a self-deceiver, and much else besides), you will miss something, something morally important about such a case, if the spectacle of Dimmesdale's suffering at the pillory – the kind of suffering that only a morally accountable being might experience – has no power to move you in the kinds of primitive ways I have described. We might put the point like this: we do not, in the kind of case I am interested in, *decide* these things – say, that we will pity Dimmesdale because it is appropriate to do so. Pity and other related responses are, rather, the background of moral responsiveness to others through which we understand what it is to be human: an understanding that makes serious moral thought as opposed to the mere practice of moral judging possible; that makes it possible for me to attend in moral judgement to the life of another.

Or, looked at from the opposite direction, they are responses that, if lacking in connection to our moral judgements of others, reveal those judgements themselves to be a hollow sham: not serious recognition of the life of another but mere moralism.

## Moral judgement and moral response

Still, it could be argued that I have not shown that there is a form of moral thought distinct from moral judgement, so learning to respond to situations in the right kind of way *is* learning to judge, which involves most fundamentally learning to see things correctly. These capacities of response enable us to recognize morally relevant features of the situation we face; they enable us to see things aright. Action then issues, we may even say issues immediately, once we see what the situation morally requires of us. In a sense I think this is perfectly correct, for I am arguing that certain capacities of response are partially constitutive of our moral understanding. My concern is not to say that there is a kind of moral thought distinct from the very idea of moral judgement *as a kind of practical ability*. Thus moral judgement, for example, could be thought of as a kind of knowing *how* (to act), as I alluded to in the previous chapter. Moral judgement here can be understood simply as the ability to respond to situations in the morally right kind of way (I myself will argue in later chapters that, for example, such capacities of response play this role in enlarging our moral sensibilities). My point is, rather, first, to say that moral thought extends beyond moral judgement understood as applying moral concepts, principles and theories to particular agents in specific situations.[12]

Nevertheless, and second, there is a sense in which the view that moral judgement amounts to seeing things aright is, I think, mistaken. For again it implies that there is some normative perspective from which the problem of moralism just disappears, that the kind of failure involved can be characterized ultimately as a kind of *cognitive* error, when what I want to argue is that at the most basic level what may be lacking is not this but what I have called a primitive capacity of response. To explain: what I want to stress is that such moral understanding – seeing things aright – occurs in the context of, and depends on, an understanding of what it is to be human that cannot be separated from certain kinds of primitive responsiveness to other human beings. So I have suggested that what is most fundamental in a case like the one I have been discussing from Hawthorne – where what is at issue is our recognition that Hester and Dimmesdale remain morally accountable beings – is not something we need first to see, in the sense that this might then *justify* what we need to do, but something that we need to do, to respond in a certain way. And a potential difference between the view I have advanced and what may be described as certain moral cognitivist theories emerges once we consider the role some such theories assign to practical reasons or, more precisely, to the idea of acting for a reason.

An idea common in a range of moral cognitivist theories is that moral action follows (perhaps immediately) once an agent sees things aright. But what that means is that the way the agent conceives of the morally salient features of the situation constitutes their reason for acting.[13] According to the view I have defended, moral agency does not *always* involve acting for such reasons. Consider the quotation from Winch, above. Winch suggests there that "one cannot (unless a very special context is supplied) ask why the fact that someone is suffering should be a *reason* for pitying him" (emphasis added). In order to see this point we must distinguish two senses of acting for a reason. According to the first sense, we might simply say, in the case of sympathy, that the reason we help someone is that they are suffering. But there is another kind of reason that might seem to be required: *a reason why that person's suffering should be a reason to help them*. According to the second sense, what is required is a reason that will justify one's actions in the special sense that it is a reason why the person's suffering is a reason to help them. Now it is this sense of acting for a reason that is operative when an agent, it is supposed, acts on the basis of, or in light of, what strikes them as the morally salient features of this situation (the relevant reason is not merely that the other suffers but that suffering is morally salient). It may be that the suffering is one morally salient feature among others, or that it is the only salient feature, but in both cases one is responding most fundamentally to one's judgement about the moral facts. My reason for action is not the brute or *natural* fact of another's suffering but the fact that it is morally salient.

Thinking in terms of the second sense of acting for a reason indicated above, we do not, in the usual kind of case, ask why the fact
that someone else is suffering is a reason for pitying him: we do not
ask for a reason in *this* sense for being so moved. (The need for such
a justification is, as I shall explain, unusual.) This is not to say that
in other (unusual) cases we cannot ask "Why do you pity him?" or
answer "Because he is suffering in such and such a way". For example,
there will be cases where we doubt that a person is really suffering
in some way: "Why do you pity him?", "Because he really is suffering the pangs of remorse, not just the loss of reputation". But there is
no question that this person is an appropriate object of pity; the issue
is only about whether this person is suffering in the requisite way on
this occasion. Both asking for and giving a reason for one's response,
on this occasion, assumes a background of responsiveness to others
according to which other human beings just are appropriate objects of
pity. And the point is that we do not pity someone in the usual kind
of case – cases where it is clear that a person is suffering in one way or
another – *because* we feel that acting in this way is justified; the need
for justification requires a special context and that is what makes such
a case unusual.

Seeing things correctly, or judging correctly, and *then* acting is tied
to the idea that one is, or may be, justified in so acting, in the sense I
have outlined above. But what I am claiming, really following Winch,
is that our moral responses to others and the world are not all about
acting for a reason in this sense, so that there is a dimension to the
moral life that extends beyond acting for such reasons or – which that
involves – making judgements about how one ought to act. To say that
moral agency *always* follows (when it does) from such judgements,
where moral judgement is cashed out in terms of seeing things aright
– seeing what is morally salient – makes the unusual cases (the ones
where justification seems called for) seem like the usual case, or rather
the only kind of case that counts as moral agency at all. But against
this consider how peculiar it is to ask, in a usual kind of case, why the
fact that someone is suffering is a reason to pity them. What are we to
say, thinking of the present case for example, to someone who in their
judgement of others reliably recognizes the wrong but *does not ever*, as
they might say, "see any reason for pity"? What don't they see? What

justifies our pity? In the usual kind of case, reasons give out, but not in the sense that there is no reason that we might give that another might accept, but in the sense that there is no reason we might give. We can say that they do not see things correctly and, as I have conceded, in a sense they do not; they miss something important about what it is to be human. Nevertheless, intended as a gesture towards something that is supposed to *justify*, say, our pity, this claim really idles. For, at least as I have argued, what comes first, what is most fundamental, is not something that we want another to *see* – which is supposedly our reason for acting – but something we want them to *do*: to pity.

Of course the obvious response to the view of our thoughts about other human beings that I have presented is to ask: what in a given situation mandates certain responses to another human being as opposed to others; in virtue of what is pity a morally appropriate response to Dimmesdale; in virtue of what are the Puritans' responses to Hester morally inappropriate? Here I would make three points; first, such a question really supposes that there is some *further* normative perspective that might justify such responses, when I am claiming that in the most basic and usual kinds of case there simply is no such perspective.[14] But, second, while our responses to other human beings, including in the kinds of contexts I have been concerned with, are unthinking and in that sense unjustified, they are, all the same, widely shared. My point is that it is in virtue of such shared responses to each other that we have the conception that we do of what it is to be and to suffer as a human being. As against this conception, some responses (or the lack of certain responses) will strike us as expressive of a failure to recognize something important about our humanity, even if we cannot characterize what someone fails to recognize independently of the very responses they appear to lack. But further, and third, to say that the shared responses at issue are unthinking is not to say that the processes through which we come to share them are entirely unreflective, and this is the point of attending to Hawthorne's novella. If our first response to Dimmesdale is *simply* to condemn him, by the end of *The Scarlet Letter* we may be moved, in turn and in equally immediate and unthinking ways, to view him quite differently. A feature of literature to which I shall return is its power to draw on our own capacities of response in order to reveal to us something of what human life is like. Thus it may be through reading *The Scarlet Letter* that we come to recognize something of what it is to be human that we might have missed.

## Conclusion

I have focused in this chapter on an extreme case of moralism. The reason for this is that in this extreme case one might see most clearly how moralism involves a failure to recognize or acknowledge, in the context of one's moral judgements, the full humanity of those one judges and, specifically, their nature as morally accountable beings. Most moralistic judgements are not so extreme. Nevertheless, the tendency to caricature, to respond in one's judgements of others in ways that display a failure to acknowledge their humanity, is present in many less extreme cases as well. Part of what makes the moralism of the Puritans of Boston so extreme is that Hester's humanity is so clearly there for all to see. Hester's fine needlework in embroidering her scarlet letter is not, as most of the townsfolk seem to think, a sign of her moral infirmity; rather, it reflects her own acknowledgment of what she has done. But many other cases will be less clear, so it may be that we suspect that a given person fails to recognize the moral significance of their wrongdoing; indeed, as I have noted, some may think this way about Dimmesdale. But even in such cases pity is still an appropriate response so long as we think that such a person remains a morally accountable being.

In such cases we may pity, for example, what another may eventually have to confront and suffer: a genuine acknowledgment of what they have done. Or we may pity them for what they have lost, even though they themselves cannot recognize its value, including a clear sense of all that it is to be a morally accountable being. And in such cases there is scope for a more everyday moralism. Consider the controversy surrounding the so-called "children overboard affair" in Australia in 2001.[15] The Australian government of the day claimed that a group of seafaring asylum-seekers had thrown their children over the side of the boat they were on in order to secure their rescue and future residency in Australia for them and their children. The moral outrage that ensued served to demonize the asylum-seekers and strengthened the case for a stricter policy in relation to asylum-seekers entering Australian waters illegally. As it turns out the claims were false; no children were thrown overboard in this incident. But what was hardly considered in the whole affair was, even assuming the claims were true, how desperate these people must have been to act in this way.

Even if the story had been true, one might have thought that the terrible actions these people had apparently been driven to might be a cause for pity. But there was very little pity along with the outrage. All the focus was rather on whether the claims were true. The point, it seems, was that we need consider these people only if the claims were false; otherwise they simply deserve our condemnation. There are of course some very difficult cases: cases where a person has behaved so monstrously and where the possibility of remorse seems so remote that we may be inclined to think that this person must be some kind of monster, somehow beyond the scope of pity. I think it is to miss something fundamental in our relations to human beings, something moreover essential to morality, to hold that another human being is ever beyond pity.[16] But I shall not argue that point here. I suggest only that a boatload of poor and desperate people seeking a better life seems a long way from such cases. The public debate in Australia over asylum-seekers, and the children overboard affair in particular, offers a real-life illustration of the distorting influence of moralism.

Moralism is not, I have contended, simply a matter of judging another too severely. It is, rather, indicated by the manner in which we judge others: by the way in which we respond to them that accompanies our specific moral judgements about them. So, in addition to judging someone even extremely severely, we might respond to them all the same with pity or mercy, for example. Further, I have suggested that this pattern of responsiveness to others indicates a dimension of moral thought that extends beyond simply making moral judgements. My discussion of moralism serves in part to highlight this wider conception of moral thought, and this is a topic I shall return to in later chapters, especially Chapter 5. One thing I shall consider there, as I have already flagged, is the role of literature in such moral thought. Here let me just conclude by saying that *The Scarlet Letter* is a work of literature that manifests precisely this kind of thought. So Hawthorne does not shy away from judging Dimmesdale extremely severely; he is,

Hawthorne tells us, a "subtle but remorseful hypocrite". But, and this is the important point, he treats Dimmesdale and all the characters in his sad tale with an understanding pity. Moreover, in so far as Hawthorne's portraits move us to pity, we might gain a sense of what moral thought really required of us beyond simply judging another. That this is part of what Hawthorne is trying to achieve with *The Scarlet Letter* is clear from the outset. As Hester is about to leave the prison on her walk to the pillory, Hawthorne writes that, by the prison portal:

> was a wild rosebush, covered, in this month of June, with its delicate gems, which might be imagined to offer their fragrance and fragile beauty to the prisoner as he went in, and to the condemned criminal as he came forth to his doom, in token that the deep heart of Nature could pity and be kind to him ... Finding it so directly on the threshold of our narrative, which is now about to issue from that inauspicious portal, we could hardly do otherwise than pluck one of its flowers and present it to the reader. It may serve, let us hope, to symbolize some sweet moral blossom, that may be found along the track, or relieve the darkening close of a tale of human frailty and sorrow. ([1850] 1960: 50)

# THREE

# Trusting oneself

In the previous chapter I considered the way in which moralism may involve a failure to recognize, in one's judgements of another person, aspects of their humanity and specifically their nature as a morally accountable being. In this chapter I want to examine how moralism, as I have characterized it, involves an *evasion* of serious or genuine moral thought and reflection, and what moralistic judgements suggest about the character of those who make them. In so doing I hope to get somewhat clearer about the kinds of demands that moral thought or reflection makes on us and thus the kinds of qualities of character that serious moral thought and judgement require. Specifically, I shall argue that moral thought in our response to morally controversial works of art involves more than simply applying our pre-existing moral ideas, concepts and principles to the work. Beyond this I shall suggest that moral thought about such works also involves attending to our own responses to the work and what they might reveal about the values at issue. Thus in this chapter I continue to elaborate the wider conception of moral thought that I have already introduced, whereas in later chapters (particularly Chapter 5) I shall examine in further detail the nature of the demands such moral thought makes on us beyond simply making moral judgements.

To begin, consider the following quotation relating a conversation between Dr Samuel Johnson and two of his admirers:

Mrs. Digby told me that when she lived in London with her sister Mrs. Brooke, they were every now and then honoured by the visits of Dr. Johnson. He called on them one day soon after the publication of his immortal dictionary. The two ladies paid him due compliments on the occasion. Amongst other topics of praise they very much commended the omission of all *naughty* words. "What! my dears! then you have been looking for them?" said the moralist. The ladies, confused at being thus caught, dropped the subject of the dictionary.

(Best 1829, quoted in Hill 1897: 390)

There is a difference, as I have already suggested, between the moralist and the moralizer, who I take to be a person who is afflicted with moralism. That Dr Johnson, for example, was a moralist as juxtaposed to a moralizer is shown not by the absence of "naughty words" in his dictionary but by his suspicion of anyone who would go looking for them. Dr Johnson's question to Mrs Digby and Mrs Brooke reminds us that we cannot always take a person's concern for morality at face value: that serious moral thought and debate, which is to say the proper activity of the moralist, requires of us something more and, as I have said, something more onerous than a mere concern for morality. In order to illustrate what more it requires I shall focus in this chapter on the recent (and extreme) moral criticism directed against the work of Australian artist Bill Henson. While the example is Australian, the controversy over Henson could easily have arisen in many other countries, including in Europe and North America. What I hope to draw from this example is something of the nature of moralism and, in contrast to this, what serious moral thought and reflection really require of us both in this case and more generally.

## The Henson case

On Thursday 22 May 2008, Australian photographer Bill Henson was to open an exhibition of new works at the Roslyn Oxley9 Gallery in Sydney. Although an international artist of some note for many years – his work is held in many major international galleries and he has represented Australia at the Venice Biennale – Henson was not widely known in Australia. By 23 May he would be front-page news. As reported in *The Australian* newspaper on 22 May, the invitation to the exhibition opening reproduced an image from the exhibition of a naked twelve-year-old girl. Similar images from the exhibition also appeared on the gallery's website.[1] The image of the girl, like other images of nude adolescents from the exhibition, was immediately condemned as obscene or sexualized in a variety of quarters. The exhibition opening was postponed and the gallery closed while police, in response to a number of complaints, decided on whether to lay charges against either the gallery or Henson. The Australian prime minister at the time, Kevin Rudd, said that the image of the girl was "absolutely revolting" and that "kids deserve to have the innocence of their childhood protected" (*Today* 2008). Morris Iemma, then premier of New South Wales, declared "I find [the images] offensive and disgusting. I don't understand why parents would agree to allow their kids to be photographed like this" (*Herald Sun*, 23 May 2008). Many in fact saw the issue of consent as the crucial one, arguing that the images in the exhibition were clearly sexualized and that as such the parents could not give consent to having their children photographed in this way. Still others claimed that the children in the images in the exhibition were exploited by Henson. In the end the government's classification board – itself made up of broadly representative members of the public – was asked to classify the offending image on the invitation. This they did, giving it a rating of PG for "parental guidance suggested" (one rating above G or "suitable for general admission") and no charges were ever pressed.[2]

In the light of the government classification board's eventual rating of the central offending image of the naked girl, many of the moral judgements made about Henson, the girl's parents and the gallery appear extraordinary and extreme. Indeed, some of Henson's defenders have accused various public and media figures of inciting a kind of moral panic. If there was an overreaction in some quarters to Henson, then perhaps that is partly explained by recent revelations about child sexual abuse in various institutions, by the extent and easy availability of child pornography on the internet and by the clandestine operations of groups of paedophiles in producing and distributing this material.

The fact that Henson's images were themselves available on the Roslyn Oxley9 Gallery website perhaps touched on community anxieties about child pornography on the internet, even though Henson's images could not plausibly be characterized as pornographic. If they could be so characterized, then an extensive retrospective of Henson's work at the State Gallery of New South Wales just a couple of years earlier would also have been widely condemned, since it included the display of similar images created by Henson over a period of thirty years. As it was, that exhibition received much critical acclaim and no public complaints. All the same, it must be said, I think, that many thoughtful people had reasonable moral concerns about some of Henson's images and I do not want to belittle those concerns. As I indicated in Chapter 1, my concern is not with whether or not there are genuine moral concerns with some of Henson images but with whether some of the moral judgements made about him at the time display the vice of moralism. It is to this issue that I now turn.

There is no doubt that in condemning Henson many commentators were concerned with morality. But the nature of some judgements suggests that many were also guilty of moralism. The more specific characteristic of moralism that I shall focus on in this chapter, and which is striking in the Henson case, is that moralism involves a failure, in an important sense, to recognize that morality is difficult. I do not mean that it is hard to follow morality's dictates, although it often is, but that morality requires the will to be scrupulously critical and honest with and about *oneself*. More important for morality than a willingness to judge others is the courage to critically examine one's own actions or responses and motivations.[3] For the moralizer, however, the situation is reversed: while the moral scrutiny of others is central for them, they almost never subject themselves to the same critical gaze. Commenting on the debate over Henson, Germaine Greer perhaps had a point in suggesting that any man who calls a picture of a naked adolescent girl "revolting" protests too much (Greer 2008: 13).[4] Or at least, and to be more precise, if a heterosexual adult male tells us in such a context that an image of a naked teenage girl is revolting *merely because she is naked*, we would be wise, much as Dr Johnson was in the example above, to be suspicious.[5] Even if we think that there is a genuine moral concern with Henson's photograph (about, say, the ethics of photographing adolescents in the nude), to put the point like that does not indicate serious moral reflection but an evasion of it.

The sort of extreme and possibly self-deceiving reaction to Henson's work indicated above only serves to obscure important distinctions we might need to make. So a frustrating aspect of the debate about Henson's photographs was that in this context one could not talk positively about the representation of human sexuality without seeming to endorse the sexualization of children. Obviously Henson's images represent human sexuality but that is not the same thing as sexualizing children. The point is so obvious it reminds me of a scene in the spoof rock documentary *This is Spinal Tap*. The band's manager informs the group that the record company will not release their new album, *Smell the Glove*, because the cover image is sexist, to which the guitarist Nigel replies, confused, "What's wrong with being sexy?" It seems that many of Henson's critics have something in common with Nigel in that they think any description with the word "sex" in it amounts to only one thing. Nigel misses the point but at least he is honest about his own motivations.

## Ern Malley

The case of Henson and the moralism it engendered is by no means unique in the history of art and censorship. Indeed, the Henson case has similarities to, and is further illuminated by, an earlier instance of moralism in Australia: the prosecution in South Australia in 1944 of Max Harris, editor of *Angry Penguins*, a modernist literary and art review, for publishing a number of allegedly obscene poems by Ern Malley. Harris must be the unluckiest literary editor of all time. Not only was Harris the victim of Australia's most famous literary hoax – Ern Malley never existed, his poetry was created by two young conservative Australian poets, Harold Stewart and James McAuley, to mock the modernist style – but he was then charged because the works were thought to be either "indecent advertisements" or "indecent, immoral or obscene".[6]

The hoaxers' point in the Ern Malley affair was to show that since, as they thought, modernist poetry was all pretentious nonsense, Harris would not be able to spot that their poems were meaningless. But the fact that the poems were meaningless was no deterrent to the police or prosecution. As Michael Heyward says in his account of the Ern Malley affair:

> the Crown case seemed to be that where the poetry was not obscene it was unintelligible, and that was almost as bad. ... [the prosecutor, D. C. Williams] sought to deny a paraphrasable content where he could detect nothing risqué, but was on the alert for meaning if the poem looked naughty.
>
> (1993: 200)

And as Heyward goes on to suggest, the magistrate, L. E. Clarke, seemed to want it both ways too. So Clarke thought that interpreting the poem "Sweet William" was "rather like attempting to unravel a crossword puzzle from a newspaper with the aid of only half the clues, and without the satisfaction of seeing the solution in the next issue" (trial transcript, quoted in *ibid*.: 208–9), yet at the same time he wanted to claim the phrase "unforgivable rape" that appears in the poem could only be referring to the actual act of rape despite the alternative interpretation Harris had offered him.

As Heyward puts it, "The *Angry Penguins* trial concluded a script which nobody without a sense of humour could have invented, and nobody with one could resist" (*ibid*.: 185). Most ridiculous, and telling, of all was the cross-examination of the arresting officer Detective Vogelesang, whose testimony, Heyward says, "brought the house down". Questioned about the meaning of the poem "Night Piece", Vogelesang had this to offer: "Apparently someone is shining a torch in the dark ... visiting through the park gates. To my mind they were going there for some disapproved motive ... I have found that people who go into parks at night go there for immoral purposes" (trial transcript, quoted in *ibid*.: 191). Vogelesang's thoughts about parks at night and the tendentious speculations of Williams and Clarke seem to have led them to see immorality where there was none except in their own imaginings. We might also wonder whether some of those who see pornography, sexualization or exploitation in Henson's images of naked adolescents see anything except the content of their own imaginings.

From our viewpoint, the concerns of the prosecution and the police in the Ern Malley case may seem laughable. Yet one thing that was driving that concern can also be seen to be driving the concern over Henson. It seems clear from the Ern Malley case that one thing that worried people was that they did not know what to think or make of Malley's poems. And that seems to be part of the problem in the Henson case as well. Henson's photographs are not obviously pornographic or obscene in the ordinary sense of those terms.[7] That, I think, explains why the debate quickly turned from the issue of obscenity to one of consent and child exploitation. But that hardly clarified matters, for to claim that the girl in Henson's photograph was exploited arguably just begs the question. If Henson's photograph was obscene or sexualized, then the girl would have been exploited by Henson. But Henson's image was not in any obvious sense obscene or sexualized; that was the original problem with accounting for many peoples' concern with it. Certainly the girl's parents actually admired Henson's work and thought that posing for Henson was a worthwhile thing for their daughter to do. But then where is the exploitation? One might claim that the parents got it wrong and that their daughter will regret the affair later in life. But children often grow up to regret or even resent some aspect of their upbringing. So a child may grow up to regret or resent being brought up in accordance with strict religious rules or practices. The issue in all such cases is not whether a child regrets or resents aspects of their upbringing but whether their rights were infringed or whether they were harmed. But any claim that this girl has been exploited or harmed is perhaps no more plausible in the end than the claim that Henson's photographs are straightforwardly obscene. Here, as in the case of Ern Malley, people were clearly troubled but were unable to adequately account for that feeling.

My main point in the preceding paragraph concerns the difficulty of accounting for people's objections to Henson's images, given that they were not in any obvious way obscene, sexualized or exploitative. But that does not dispose of the argument from consent. For according to one way of reading that argument, what we make of Henson's images, including whether or not we find them morally disturbing, is *irrelevant*; the crucial issue is that children cannot consent to be photographed in this way for public display.[8] However, the problem with this objection is in characterizing what we might mean in saying that children cannot consent to being photographed *in this way*. Since the photographs were not in any obvious and agreed sense obscene, sexualized or exploitative, what might this mean? One suggestion would be that our naked bodies are a very private kind of thing and that it is the responsibility of parents to protect the privacy of their children. So one might argue that Henson's images are an invasion of children's privacy. I do not want to deny that respect for privacy is an important moral value. The point is, though, that not everyone saw Henson's images as an invasion of privacy in this way. What is at issue, what is in contention, is the moral meaning or significance of child nudity in art. So we are not thinking here of a case in which there is an obvious wrongdoing in *producing* the work, such as if the child were tricked into taking off their clothes. While this is obviously exploitative, in the case of Henson the issue is: is it an invasion of privacy and so exploitative to photograph adolescents or children in the nude if both the children and their parents consent? The question remains as to how we are to reach a judgement in this kind of case.

Here is one way of thinking of moral thought and judgement. In order to reach a judgement about Henson's images of nude adolescents we apply to them our existing moral ideas, concepts and principles – for example, about privacy and consent – and those ideas, concepts and principles will determine whether Henson's photographs are morally objectionable or even ought not to have been produced. While I do not deny that in assessing a work of art it is appropriate to bring such moral conceptions to bear, what I do deny is that this is all there is to moral thought and judgement in a case like this. For if someone does not see Henson's images as a kind of invasion of privacy, then for them the issue may turn on a very different conception of the moral meaning or significance of children being photographed like this. If someone else judges that this is an invasion of privacy, the response will be, "Just look at the image themselves, then you might be inclined to think differently about the sort of thing you want to say is an invasion of privacy". Of course, even if a particular person were to accept that invitation they might still not be convinced, and there may be nothing wrong in that. What is a mistake, however, is to think what we make of Henson's photographs if we do attend to them is irrelevant to the moral concerns at issue.[9]

The conception of moral thought and judgement that I am objecting to here focuses exclusively on the application of our existing moral ideas, concepts and principles to works of art, and discounts entirely the possibility that a work of art – through what it might reveal about a whole range of human values – might lead us to reassess and modify the very moral ideas, concepts and principles we are applying to it. To say that what we make of the work, what we find revealed or revealing in it, is irrelevant to the moral judgements we might then make about it, is to deny outright that art might play this kind of role in our moral thought and judgement.

Consider the issue of privacy and the kind of moral significance we might attach to that. Our moral concern with privacy is not just about nudity but extends to forms of human intimacy. A general moral concern we might have is about art when its aim is precisely to portray intimate private moments. My point is that what we think about the portrayal of such a moment may depend on the work itself, the way in which the artist deals with his subject. One of my own favourite pictures is Rembrandt's painting of his lover Hendrickje Stoffels bathing. Hendrickje is not naked but the portrait displays a very private moment all the same; the picture is an extremely revealing – and tender – portrayal of Hendrickje's distinct human vulnerability. On that point, it has been speculated that the painting had a specific personal significance for Rembrandt, because the year it was painted Hendrickje had suffered public humiliation for becoming pregnant to Rembrandt without being married to him. While this work may raise issues about privacy, our judgement is going to be based not on some prior conception of the moral significance of privacy but on Rembrandt's treatment of his theme. Rembrandt's treatment of his theme is what makes this paining something other than, say, a piece of voyeurism.

My point above is not to skew the debate about Henson in his favour by comparing his work to an artist of Rembrandt's stature; it is just to say that the place certain moral concerns, say, about privacy and the portrayal of what is intimate, have in our assessment of a work of art may depend on the way in which an artist deals with such moral concerns within the work itself. It may be that Henson's treatment of the morally contentious issue of child nudity in his art is a failure in these terms. My point is just that whether we think that turns in part on what we make of the works themselves, not simply on the application of our pre-existing moral ideas, say about privacy, to the work.

## Art and ambiguity

I do not want to deny that Henson's images of naked or semi-naked adolescents are in a way disturbing. But if we are to avoid moralism here, we need to ask ourselves why. I remember the first time I saw Henson's photographs; it was at an exhibition in Melbourne in the 1980s. In some of the works in that exhibition Henson had juxtaposed images (characteristically dark and sometimes squalid) of naked or semi-naked street kids with images of grand interiors. I found these images hard to look at.[10] In these photographs, as in many of his later photographs of adolescents, there is a disturbing *ambiguity*, by which I mean that they are apt to produce conflicting responses in the viewer. As John McDonald observes in his excellent review of Henson's 1980s photographs, "Henson leaves the viewer with an unbearable dilemma. Is this an exercise in gruesome voyeurism or social comment? ... This dangerous and difficult ambiguity seems central to the experience of Henson's work" (1988: 91). But it is precisely this sort of ambiguity, and the consequent lack of simple or obvious moral meaning or purpose, that many people find so offensive about Henson's work and much other artistic achievement as well.

To illustrate, consider another morally contentious work with which Henson's photographs were compared during the controversy: Nabokov's novel *Lolita* ([1955] 1995). Attempts to defend Henson by making comparisons with Nabokov's great novel may fail because many people regard *Lolita* as morally objectionable for much the same reasons as they find Henson's photographs of naked adolescents objectionable. For Nabokov's book is ambiguous too; in fact it is multiply ambiguous – this story of a paedophile's obsession with a twelve-year-old girl is variously shocking, poignant and even funny. And one objection is that a book on such a subject ought not to be funny; being funny, it may be thought, counts against it being shocking in a morally edifying sort of way. According to a certain, moralistic, turn of mind, if you are going to tell a story about a paedophile or photograph adolescents nude you had better have a clear and unambiguous moral purpose. So according to this way of thinking it may be acceptable to, say, photograph a naked adolescent running in terror from her napalmed village but only because such a photograph openly serves a noble cause.

Considering the above point, the case of *Lolita* is apposite partly because Nabokov, in his afterword to the novel, denies that it has anything moral to teach us. As he says, "For me a work of fiction exists only insofar as it affords me what I shall bluntly call aesthetic bliss" (*ibid.*: 358). Nabokov's apparent distinction between moral and aesthetic value and his lauding of the latter and eschewing of the former may seem to some to make *Lolita* all the more obviously morally objectionable. In his own defence Nabokov suggests that the refusal of several publishers to buy the book "was based not on my treatment of the theme but on the theme itself" (*ibid.*: 357), and he thinks the claim of immorality levelled at *Lolita* is absurd. But many object precisely to his treatment of the theme, on the aesthetic bliss that emerges from or is intertwined with rank depravity. Consider how Humbert Humbert begins his confessional narrative: "Lolita, light of my life, fire of my loins. My sin, my soul. Lo-lee-ta: the tip of the tongue taking a trip of three steps down the palate to tap, at three, on the teeth. Lo. Lee. Ta" (*ibid.*: 7). Many people have noted how we, as readers, are invited to savour these first lines. They are very carefully crafted. Of particular note is the way Nabokov is drawing our attention to the sound of the words. As Derek Attridge says:

> The extravagant aural patterning of the first two sentences induces a strong consciousness of the sounds as sounds, and the third sentence then draws attention to the goings-on within the mouth, producing an acute awareness of the tongue-tip's action in pronouncing *t* and *th* eighteen times in twenty-two words. The pleasure to be derived from this bravura performance is not that of a precise piece of description, but that of a showman's trick, and its function is to alert us to the narrator's fascination with and expertise in language, his fusion of verbal and sexual delight. (Attridge 1981: 234)

But the problem is that the pleasure we derive from reading these words and imagining all the "goings-on within the mouth" is also in the context extremely shocking. We know that Humbert is a paedophile and that Lolita is his victim. What Humbert is doing is rolling around in his mouth his pet name for a twelve-year-old girl. It is the fusion of verbal and sexual delight in this context that is shocking and which may make us recoil from the very pleasure we experience as we read. Nabokov's aesthetic achievement is hard to deny – this is indeed a "bravura performance" – but that, some will say, only makes these lines more morally objectionable.

However, before we can condemn Nabokov's treatment of his theme we need to attend to the complex nature of our response to *Lolita*, and even to these first lines, for there is both pleasure *and* revulsion in reading them. It is simply too crude, for example, to suggest that Nabokov is asking us to share sympathetically the desires of a paedophile. Of course we don't sympathise; we know from Nabokov's mock introduction by psychiatrist "Dr John Ray, Jr, PhD" that this is the narrative of a sexual pervert. Yet the aesthetic pleasure is important. First, the lyric beauty of these lines prevents us from simply dismissing Humbert as a monster; a monster he may be, but the beauty and eloquence of Humbert's expression of his desire is nonetheless affecting and we are thus engaged with Humbert's narrative. Second, we notice through this pleasure and beyond Humbert's desire, as Attridge says, "the narrator's fascination with and expertise in language, his fusion of verbal and sexual delight". What becomes clear is that this fusion in which Humbert's desire for, and to possess, Lolita is conflated with the pleasure he takes in language expresses, indeed helps to constitute, Humbert's blindness with respect to Lolita: his inability to see her for who she really is. Nabokov has said, also in his afterword to *Lolita*, that his "initial shiver of inspiration was somehow prompted by a newspaper story about an ape ... who, after months of coaxing by a scientist, produced the first drawing ever charcoaled by an animal: this sketch showed the bars of the poor creature's cage" (Nabokov [1955] 1995: 353). Humbert's narrative, as Nabokov himself has elsewhere suggested, is Humbert "drawing and shading and erasing and redrawing the bars of his cage" (Nabokov 1955): the cage that separates him from the rest of humanity and most of all from Lolita. The very made-up name "Lolita" illustrates this point: this name is given for the sound of it; it has everything to do with Humbert's desire, the fusion of verbal and sexual delight indicated above, and almost nothing to do with the living girl Dolores Haze. But the author of *Lolita* is Vladimir Nabokov, not Humbert Humbert, and we see Lolita for who she is; we, as it were, see through the bars of Humbert's cage. Despite Humbert's evasions, lies and trickery with language, Lolita's humanity nevertheless becomes clearly visible to us.

Nabokov tells us in his afterword that he is not a writer of didactic fiction, and that "*Lolita* has no moral in tow" ([1955] 1995: 358). But that is not to say that there is nothing that we might learn, including about ourselves, through a novel such as *Lolita*. It is worth noting, for instance, that while Nabokov declares his interest in fiction is only in aesthetic bliss he goes on to describe such a state as "a sense of being somehow, somewhere, connected with other states of being where art (curiosity, tenderness, kindness, ecstasy) is the norm" (*ibid.*). So Nabokov is hardly denying some moral dimension to art or the power of art to illuminate human life in some sense. In some cases art, including literature, can wear its moral purpose on its sleeve: Hogarth's *A Rake's Progress* and Charles Dickens's *Hard Times*, along with some of his other novels, are examples. But art, including literature, does not always serve morality or truth in such an openly didactic way. It may even be that an artist has no very clear conception of what (if any[11]) specific ideas, values or claims they want to convey – artists are not essayists – and that their work is itself a way of working that out. In that case, all an artist can do is trust in that particular mode of responsiveness to the world that is manifest in their work. And the viewer (or reader) faces a similar challenge; we too may need to trust in our own potentially conflicting responses to the artist's work, to accept them and to be willing to learn from them. This brings me back to moralism, for it is characteristic of a kind of moralizer that he does not trust his own responses; he does not, even if he is not consciously aware of it, trust himself.

We can see now what was more or less implicit in the Ern Malley trial: why ambiguity *itself* is so offensive to such a moralizer. This moralizer wants to know what the work is about so that he can respond (morally) appropriately, but in a particular case it may be that we only come to understand the meaning (or meanings) of a work through our responses to it. We have to be open to such responses *whatever they may be*. The moralizer though is unable or unwilling to be open in this way. That may be because the moralizer is unable to accept the responsibility that such openness entails. If he condemns child nudity in art, it is perhaps not because he believes he will find the image of a naked teenager revolting but because, and notwithstanding his denials, he is worried he might not. Or if he is disgusted at the very fact or idea that such photographs are produced, it may not be his fear for children that is driving him but maybe his fear for himself. But at many other times a moralizer's lack of openness may indicate simply a fear that with only his own responses to go by he may not know what to think when he feels that he *should* know, or (what this amounts to) a want of confidence in his *own* judgement as mediated by those very responses.

## Art and moral reflection

What the moralizer misses in relation to art (but not just in relation to art) is what we might learn through our various responses to the work (as to the world). To illustrate, an important feature of art, as I have already noted, is that it may produce a number of *conflicting* responses in us. Think again, for example, of McDonald's review of Henson. Looking at Henson's photographs of young people we *may* derive a voyeuristic pleasure. But at the same time the reference to this mode of viewing in the work itself – Henson uses low directional light, which seems to draw his subjects out of the darkness – not to mention the overall level of abstraction of the images is apt to produce in one an unsettling consciousness of this very pleasure, which may then undercut it: the taste, as it were, turning to dust in one's mouth. And that conflict, a conflict at the level of immediate response, may be the point. It is perhaps through this kind of conflict that the work is illuminating. So Henson's images do not endorse voyeuristic tendencies or responses; they play such responses off against other conflicting responses, thereby exposing and undermining the voyeuristic gaze.

Let me stress that to acknowledge that a viewer may derive some kind of voyeuristic pleasure from Henson's photographs of naked and semi-naked adolescents is not to concede – what I have in fact denied – that such images are, after all, sexualized. Consider Henson's image of the naked twelve-year-old at the heart of the recent controversy. One reason any voyeuristic pleasure a viewer derives from this image would be disturbing is that the image *truthfully* represents adolescent sexuality; it does not – as a sexual*ized* image would – represent her as something that she is not. If the image had lied, then of course a viewer deriving a specifically *sexual* voyeuristic pleasure[12] from it might complain that they were tricked into seeing the girl as having the kind of sexuality that a twelve-year-old girl could not have, which is to give the viewer grounds for condemning Henson and excusing their pleasure. But *this* image does not lie, so the viewer must examine and take responsibility for their particular responses to it.[13] In so far as there is a reference to voyeurism in Henson's work it functions in part as an invitation to do just that. This is hardly child exploitation but it can, as I say, make for an uncomfortable experience for the *viewer*.

Consider another example of how the possible response of the viewer may be not just undercut but turned on its head by a work of art. In discussing Leni Riefenstahl's Nazi propaganda film *Triumph of the Will*, Folke Isaksson and Leif Furhammar comment on the way the viewer is "not only called upon to observe the crowd's enthusiastic reactions to its leader … but also forced into a state of participation" (Isaksson & Furhammar 1977: 392). Yet, as they go on to say, while "the suggestive power of crowds in films may be quite overwhelming … it is surprisingly easy for a commentator to undo the effect – not just minimising it but actually reversing it" (*ibid.*). So they suggest, for example, that in the British propaganda film *These are the Men* (1943), in which sequences of Riefenstahl's film are given a hostile English commentary with words by Dylan Thomas, "the enthusiasm of the mass constitutes a sounding board, but … for emotions that are directed *against* all that the mass stands for" (*ibid.*: 393). In *These are the Men* we can see how art can reveal what is corrupt or corrupting in a particular moral viewpoint, in this case the moral viewpoint of the Nazis.[14] This is just one further example of the complex ways in which a work of art may exploit our capacities of response in illuminating, including morally illuminating, ways. But it also illustrates again how our assessment of a work of art may depend on the way, and how successfully, it exploits those capacities, and that is not an assessment that can be made in advance of one's open-minded experience of the work.

The problem of moralism in relation to art might be put like this: the moralizer insists on assessing the work from what they take to be the point of view of morality or in what they think are moral terms. But in so far as they deny, distrust or are otherwise unwilling to reflect on their own responses to the work, the "moral" point of view from which they assess it remains a fundamentally impoverished one. This is not to say that one must endorse, say, one's first response to a work, but to suggest that one must at least be open to reflection on such responses. Our responses to a given work of art might surprise and disturb us; nevertheless, I contend that these responses are an essential constituent of moral thought and reflection. What is disturbing in art can show us much, for example, about the nature of human desire and our fear of that desire, about our humanity and our avoidance of it.

## Conclusion

I have *not* suggested that there can be no serious moral objections to the work of Bill Henson. My aim has been rather to show what serious moral reflection on work *like this* requires of us; my concern is with moralism in response to art not with all that might be said (morally) for or against the work of any particular artist.[15] In more general terms, nothing I have said is to deny what is surely obvious: that some art may be obscene or that in its production it may involve the exploitation of children.[16] My point though is that we cannot always *read-off* whether a work of art is obscene or exploitative or otherwise morally objectionable simply by attending to certain general facts or moral considerations. So, thinking of Henson, for example, it is a mistake to think that one can determine in advance of viewing a work of art – and on independent moral grounds – that it exploits children simply because it involves child nudity, or because some viewer may see in it nothing but an opportunity for sexual voyeurism.[17] For I claim that whether or not that charge is appropriate – or, beyond that narrow question, whether or not the work provides valuable (even moral) insights of its own – may only be revealed by what we might make of the work through our various responses to it.

In more general terms, to think that moral ideas or principles *always* settle the question of whether a work of art is morally objectionable – settle the question, that is to say, *in advance* of what might be revealed through our responses to the work – is to suppose that art itself cannot have anything independently illuminating to say about morality, or at least our conception of it. But that, I am suggesting, and as I shall explore in greater detail in the following chapters, is simply false. It is true that morality might reveal a work of art to be obscene; but it is equally true that art may reveal a particular moral point of view to be impoverished or moralistic. It may even be – as we can see from the example of *These are the Men* – that art may bring home to us how a moral point of view is fundamentally corrupt. However, that is something we may not see unless we are willing to reflect on our various, potentially conflicting, responses to particular works: to consider openly what such responses say, not so much about the artist, but about us. But there is a further point I would make here. The conception of morality implicit in the thought at the start of this paragraph itself depends on a particular – and I think problematic – idea of the place and authority of morality in our lives. According to this conception of morality, *all other values* – be they aesthetic or otherwise – are ultimately subject to morality's unrestricted authority. This view, I shall argue in the next chapter, leads to the distortion of our proper understanding of other human values and their place in our lives.

But to return to Henson, many would agree, despite all that I have said, with Melbourne philosopher John Armstrong, who, commenting on Henson, suggests "the fact that a great many profoundly decent people hate what [Henson] has done should carry weight" (2008: 14). I am not suggesting that we should ignore such responses, but I am suggesting that deciding whether we should give such offence weight requires us to reflect on the underlying motives for it. We need to ask ourselves why certain images (like Henson's) are disturbing to us; we need to reflect on the *meaning* of our responses here.[18] In Chapter 2 I argued that certain responses to other people were primitive in the sense of being immediate and explanatorily basic, but this is not to say that our immediate responses to other people (or to situations) are never open to question in any sense. So, what my discussion of this chapter aims to show is that the meaning of our own immediate responses to people and situations will sometimes not be clear or apparent to us, and that on occasion we may need to accept the invitation provided by others to consider the meaning of those responses. In such cases others may know better than us the meaning of those responses and thus see our motivations more clearly than we do ourselves. Consider, for example, the case of Emma in Jane Austen's novel of the same name. When Emma discovers that it is Mr Knightley that is the object of her new friend Harriet's affections, she does not understand, as we do, the meaning of her distress at this idea: specifically, that she herself is in love with Mr Knightley. This chapter has really been a kind of invitation to reflect on the meaning of our possible responses of moral offence and disgust at Henson's images of naked adolescents, to consider the possibility that they may be rather more complex and opaque to us than we might imagine. I shall examine this general issue again in Chapter 5, where I consider how, in another context, a person's inability to reflect on the meaning of their actions amounts to a failure of moral thought and moral understanding so serious that it morally ruins their life.

To return to Armstrong, he does at least concede that sometimes a "society needs to witness disturbing and upsetting ideas for its own good", but he thinks "this rationale has little place in liberal democracies" (2008: 14). I am inclined to think otherwise. In the same article Armstrong notes approvingly Goethe's decision not to publish a few crude poems so as not to give offence to "good people", and suggests that Henson should follow Goethe's example. But good people in the matter of what they hate or what offends them can go badly wrong, especially when that hate is directed against the representation of uncomfortable truths. There is a famous story about a descendent of one of Goethe's "good people", a Nazi officer in the occupying forces in Paris, who, while visiting Picasso in his apartment, pointed to a picture of *Guernica* and asked "Did you do that?", to which Picasso is said to have replied "No, you did". Picasso's image of the horrors of war is certainly disturbing and upsetting. But are we so much more confident that we, unlike people living in Europe in the 1930s, do not need to see it? To be unwilling to face and to reflect sometimes on what one finds upsetting or offensive is to fail to attempt to understand oneself, and certainly to fail to attempt to understand one's motivations. If art is sometimes disturbing, then it can be because it has the power to draw from us, and thus reveal to us, as I have said, much about the nature of human desire and our fear of that desire, about our humanity and our avoidance of it. But moral thought or reflection demands precisely that we face such desire along with our fear of it. Engagement with art, here specifically through attending to our responses to it, thus involves precisely the kind of difficult moral thought that decent people ignore at their peril.

# FOUR

# Overweening morality

So far I have been focusing on particular moralistic judgements, on the nature of such judgements (Chapters 1 and 2) and about what such judgements suggest about the character of those who make them (Chapter 3). So my concern so far has been with certain ways in which particular moral judgements may be flawed, or suggest character flaws, in various ways. However, there is in fact a more radical position we might take according to which the focus of criticism is not particular moral judgements but rather the whole practice of moral judgement as we might understand it. According to this view, and again in some pejorative sense, what is moralistic is a certain conception (or conceptions) of morality. The focus of criticism here is not just one particular moral theory, but our idea of morality construed much more broadly. So, Bernard Williams has argued in a number of places against what he calls "the morality system", which, with its focus on a particular notion of moral obligation, he takes as excluding other ethical considerations.[1] For Williams there is a contrast between morality, by which he means the morality system, and ethics, which he understands much more broadly and which is inclusive of ideas that we owe to a much older ethical viewpoint that comes to us from the ancient Greeks. Williams's hope is that by pointing out what he takes to be the many mistakes in *morality* he might motivate a conception of the *ethical* that is consistent with living a fully human life, something the morality system as he sees it makes problematic.

The claims by Williams and a number of other contemporary philosophers that prevailing theories of morality are moralistic are admittedly distinct from my own claims about moralism. These distinct claims are, however, connected, as I shall now begin to explain. In the most general terms, arguments that particular moral theories are moralistic tend to focus on two distinct though related ideas. First, it has been argued that the relevant moral theories, or perhaps just general moral claims or positions, are too demanding. Second, it has been argued that such moral theories trespass into areas of human life in which they should have no authority to judge as compared with demands outside morality; earlier I called such trespass morality's overweening in our lives. This second argument, which I alluded to at the end of the previous chapter, is broader than the first and really concerns the scope and limits of moral thought and judgement quite generally. It is this second kind of argument that I shall focus on in this chapter, since the particular problem of moral demandingness can itself be seen as one aspect of the broader problem of what we should understand as the proper scope and limits of morality more generally. Concerning the second problem, the tendency of morality to – as I am putting it – overween in our lives is present even in certain responses to the problem of moral demandingness. Or so I shall argue.[2]

The arguments indicated above connect to my previous discussion of moralism as follows. Whereas I have so far been concerned to explain moralism as a distortion of moral thought and reflection, in what follows I shall consider the related distortion that occurs where reflection and judgement on important human values *quite generally* are necessarily seen as subject to the findings of *a certain conception of moral reflection and judgement*. To put the point another way, while in previous chapters I have been concerned with kinds of distortion *of* morality, what I shall be concerned with in this chapter is kinds of distortion *by* morality; more precisely, I shall be concerned with the ways in which a certain conception of morality itself has the potential to distort our understanding of important human values. Such a conception is really a distorted conception of morality in that it involves, in ways we shall see, taking some things as a moral matter, a matter at least in need of moral appraisal, when they really are not. Of course moralizers need not subscribe to the kind of conception of morality that concerns me in this chapter, and those who do subscribe to such a conception need not be guilty of moralism in their everyday particular moral judgements. Nevertheless, the tendency internal to what I am calling overweening morality to see some things as moral matters when they are not can lead directly to the kind of *particular* moralistic judgements that have concerned me in previous chapters. Thus, as we shall see later, there can be a tendency internal to such overweening morality to raise moral concerns about, for example, art when they are really out of place. A tendency to see morality as having *this* place in our lives fosters the vice of moralism as I understand it. Further, a common characteristic of overweening morality and the more everyday and personal tendency to moralism in one's particular moral judgements is an unreasonable focus on *moral judgement* at the expense of other modes of thought about, or responsiveness to, the world or our own humanity. This later point I explore in depth in Chapter 5, where I examine the role of literature as a mode of moral thought.

## Impartial morality

Perhaps the most influential and sustained argument for the claim that certain moral theories or positions are moralistic is offered by Williams, in particular, in his paper "Persons, Character and Morality" (1981a). I shall consider his arguments here in some detail in this chapter. But in order to adequately assess Williams's argument one has to understand the context in which it is offered, for the context in which his arguments are given might obscure their more general point. Williams frames his argument as a response to impartial morality. His particular targets are contemporary versions of utilitarianism and Kantianism and his point is that neither kind of theory can adequately accommodate what he calls a person's "ground projects". Such projects, so Williams argues, provide "the motive force which propels [a person] into the future, and gives him a reason for living" (*ibid.*: 13).

Williams, by way of clarification, makes a number of points about these projects. First, the frustration of such a project does not mean that an agent would have to, or think he has to, commit suicide. As he says, "Other things, or the mere hope of other things, may keep him going".

Second, we generally do not have one separable ground project; rather, "there is a nexus of projects ... and it would be the loss of all or most of them that would remove meaning". Third, ground projects "do not have to be selfish, in the sense that they are just concerned with things for the agent. Nor do they have to be self-centred, in the sense that the creative projects of a Romantic artist could be considered self-centred". Indeed, such projects can be "altruistic, and in a very evident sense moral, projects". So dedicating yourself to helping the desperately poor can easily count as a ground project. Fourth, there is, Williams says:

> no contradiction in the idea of a man's dying for a ground project – quite the reverse, since if death really is necessary for the project, then to live would be to live with it unsatisfied, something which, if it really is his ground project, he has no reason to do. (*Ibid.*)

Fifth, even altruistic or moral ground projects can come into conflict with impartial morality so, as he says, a "selfless concern for justice may do havoc to quite other commitments" (*ibid.*: 14).

So what is the problem for impartial morality with such ground projects? As Williams goes on to argue:

> A man who has such a ground project will be required by Utilitarianism to give up what it requires in a given case just if that conflicts with what he is required to do as an impersonal utility-maximizer ... But the Kantian, who can do rather better than that, still cannot do well enough. For impartial morality, if the conflict really does arise, must be required to win; and that cannot necessarily be a reasonable demand on the agent. There can come a point at which it is quite unreasonable for a man to give up, in the name of the impartial good ordering of the world of moral agents, something which is a condition of his having any interest in being around in that world at all. (*Ibid.*)

Williams's argument, as I say, has as its target impartial morality, and the point he is making is that the theories to which he refers make unreasonable demands on us. Of course it need not follow from what Williams says that there is not *any* sense of impartiality that is sometimes relevant in our practical deliberations; for example, in my deliberations about how I ought to act, it is surely important in *some* context that I view myself essentially as one person among many. Williams's target is impartial moral *theories*, and his concern, as we shall see, is with the scope of the authority they assume for themselves. However, to consider a different point, one might argue that, notwithstanding the above remarks from Williams, morality does all the same make severe demands on us, demands that many of us simply fail to live up to. A particular case in point is the demands that are placed on us in the affluent First World by the need of those suffering desperate poverty and deprivation in the Third World. The question that we might then seem to face is: how much morally ought we to do to help alleviate extreme poverty and deprivation? Here again the problem of moral demandingness may re-emerge since it is consistent with having the ground projects that Williams discusses that we may be required to give up much that currently gives us fulfilment in our lives, and certainly to make sacrifices in our lives that most us have not even contemplated.

## Moral demandingness and moral permission

To illustrate how the problem of moral demandingness is not so easily disposed of, consider the following opening lines of Garrett Cullity's *The Moral Demands of Affluence*:

> Anyone who makes some effort to acquaint him- or herself with what the world is like will soon appreciate that, for many millions of people who live outside the cocoon of security and comfort that we enjoy, it is horrible: a wasteland of suffering, deprivation, and injustice. (Cullity 2004: 1)

The facts to which Cullity draws our attention invite the question that is the focus of his book: how much ought we to do to help others in such desperate need? The problem though – the problem of moral demandingness – is that meeting our obligations here may seem to require each of us, as Cullity notes, to "renounce spending on practically all of the things from which we currently get enjoyment and fulfilment" (*ibid*.: 2). While some accept this outcome (see Singer 1972; Kagan 1989; Unger 1996), others, including Cullity, find it absurd. Cullity's book is an attempt to show why we should reject what he calls the Extreme Demand – that is, giving up practically everything that gives us enjoyment or fulfilment – at the same time as recognizing the justified demand of the desperately poor for our aid. In doing so Cullity considers that the right place to look for a reply to the challenge of the Extreme Demand is along the lines that Williams envisages. What I shall argue, however, is that the kind of response to the extreme demand that Cullity pursues itself falls into the same moralistic distortions that Williams is highlighting in "Persons, Character and Morality".

Cullity's response to the problem of Extreme Demand involves arguing that "the Extreme Demand can be rejected from an appropriately impartial point of view" (Cullity 2004: 112). In particular, Cullity's argument is that "[c]ertain forms of personal partiality are themselves impartially acceptable; and they include forms of personal partiality that the Extreme Demand cannot allow for" (*ibid*.: 128). Cullity proceeds by asking two questions.

> Which kinds of life can be shown, by means of an argument of the form used against the Extreme Demand, to be ones that it is morally permissible to live? And within those lives, which goods is it morally permissible to pursue, according to an argument of this form? (*Ibid*.: 147–8)

Now the forms of partiality that are impartially acceptable, and hence the forms of life and goods that it is morally permissible to live or pursue, include certain personal relationships and projects or commitments. In this Cullity is, as he says, following Williams, who takes it that "a commitment or involvement with a particular other person might be one of the kinds of project which figured basically in a man's life in the ways already sketched" (Williams 1981a: 16). In going on to talk about the life or the goods it is *permissible* to live or pursue, however, Cullity departs from Williams. Moreover, in so doing Cullity does not really consider a further point about moralism that Williams wants to make, a point that shows how Cullity's own response to the Extreme Demand again involves a kind of moralism as Williams understands it, as I shall now explain.

## One thought too many

In "Persons, Character and Morality", Williams quotes from what he calls the "richly moralistic" account of Kantian morality given by D. A. J. Richards in his *A Theory of Reasons for Action*. In this account Richards posits, as one principle of supererogation that would be accepted in some original position of the kind envisaged by John Rawls:

> a principle of mutual love requiring that people should not show personal affection and love to others on the basis of arbitrary physical characteristics alone, but rather on the basis of traits of personality and character related to acting on moral principles.          (Quoted in Williams 1981a: 16)

Williams responds that this:

> righteous absurdity is no doubt to be traced to a feeling that love, even based on "arbitrary physical characteristics", is something which has enough power and even authority to conflict badly with morality unless it can be brought within it from the beginning.          (*Ibid.*: 16)

Williams accepts that the possibility of conflict is sound. What he questions is whether the conflict can really be resolved in the way that such Kantians and also utilitarians propose. The issue relates to possible conflicts between personal demands and impartial moral demands, and an obvious example is that of friendship. As already discussed, one way in which we may characterize a moral theory as too demanding is if it requires us to sacrifice such personal relationships or, to take another example, personal projects that are not only important to us but that, as Williams says, give us a reason to go on living at all. But that is not all there is to Williams's point. For his point is also about how impartial moral thinking *resolves* the conflict between moral and non-moral demands. As Williams says:

> There can also be conflict with moral demands *on how the outcome is arrived at*: the situation may not have been subjected to an impartial process of resolution, and this fact itself may cause unease to the impartial moral consciousness.
>
> (*Ibid.*: 17, emphasis added)

By way of illustration of the kind of unease he has in mind, Williams cites the following passage from Charles Fried's *An Anatomy of Values*. Fried worries that:

> surely it would be absurd to insist that if a man could, at no risk or cost to himself, save one or two persons in equal peril, and one of those in peril was, say, his wife, he must treat both equally, perhaps by flipping a coin. One answer is that where the potential rescuer occupies no office such as that of captain of a ship … the occurrence of the accident may itself stand as a sufficient randomizing event to meet the dictates of fairness, so he may prefer his friend, or loved one.
>
> (Quoted in Williams 1981a: 17)

Williams's interest in this passage is with the idea that this person stands in need of a *justification* for choosing to save his wife (rather than, say, just tossing a coin). What seems required by this way of thinking, suggests Williams, is a moral principle "yielding the conclusion that in situations of this kind it is at least all right (morally permissible) to save one's wife" (*ibid.*: 18). But as he goes on to say:

> [T]his construction provides the agent with one thought too many: it might have been hoped by some (for instance, by his wife) that his motivating thought, fully spelled out, would be the thought that it was his wife, not that it was his wife and that in situations of this kind it is permissible to save one's wife.
>
> (*Ibid.*)

The above objection applies to any moral theory or approach that attempts to resolve the potential conflict between the demands placed on us by just anyone (for aid, say) and the kind of demands indicated by personal relationships and projects by, as Williams says, bringing the latter into morality from the beginning, for example as permissions of various kinds. But Cullity, in his response to the Extreme Demand, takes up just such an approach. Cullity rejects the Extreme Demand by reference to the kinds of personal relationships and commitments Williams has discussed. But as Cullity sees it, it is the moral *permissibility* of these relationships and projects that show us the Extreme Demand can be rejected.[3] Indeed, as Cullity says right from the start, his book (certainly itself an important personal project) "attempts to justify the activity of writing that book" (2004: viii). But to talk in this way of the permissibility of writing a philosophical book, let alone the permissibility of spending time with and on friends and loved ones, is again to have one thought too many.[4]

One might put the point this way: what is important in negotiating the demands of morality with the demands placed on me by my personal relationships and projects is not just that there is a place for partiality – as Cullity himself notes, partiality may itself be defended on impartial grounds.[5] Moreover, Cullity does not defend a purely impartial account of morality; he does not identify morality with the impartial point of view. But, and here is what is important, that does not dispose of Williams's "one thought too many" objection. For Cullity does still accept the challenge posed by the Extreme Demand, a demand that follows from impartial morality. So Cullity thinks there is a question about whether, in the world as it is, the friendships, other relationships and personal projects that are so fundamental to our lives are morally permissible. But to wonder about that, to have that thought, is, I think Williams would say, to have one thought too many, or so I am arguing.

Suppose someone objected at this point that it is consistent with thinking of our personal relationships and projects as permissible that, when it comes to, say, spending time with a friend, our motivating thought fully spelled out is simply that we enjoy their company. Samuel Scheffler makes this point in reply to Williams's "one thought too many" objection. As he says:

It is implausible to suppose that, in general, whenever one makes a favorable assessment of the moral permissibility of an act, one is committed to saying that the agent who performs the act ought to have, and ought in part to be motivated by, the thought of its permissibility. (1992: 22)

What Scheffler says here is fair enough, however the context in which Williams made his reply to Fried is one where the impartial moral consciousness is *uneasy* with the way in which a conflict has been resolved. So the context is one in which a man wants to give preference to his wife and save her rather than a stranger but where that causes him unease. This unease suggests that something else is needed here, and that is provided by the thought that, in situations like this, it is permissible to save one's wife. Williams's point is then that such unease is in the nature of impartial moral consciousness. This is not to say that the impartial moral consciousness will always, or very often even, impinge on our practical deliberations. But, given the place impartial moral consciousness presumes to play in our lives, conflict is inevitable – it is inevitable that questions will arise about whether the forms of partiality present in our lives are morally permissible – and it is important, on this view, that impartial moral consciousness guides our actions here. When, in the kind of situation Fried envisages, the question comes up "What ought I to do?", in so far as we accept the role of impartial moral consciousness in our lives that Williams has outlined, it has to make some difference to what we do that this consciousness tells us that it is permissible (or not) to act in some way.

Returning now to Cullity, it is true that he can acknowledge, for example, that the reason we spend time with a friend is perhaps that we enjoy their company but, given his own commitment to something like impartial moral consciousness, he also wants to determine whether it is permissible to act in this kind of way, and to the extent that that matters it must in a general way motivate him to some extent at least; that such an action is or is not permissible indicates a more general practical consideration that *applies* to his decision about whether to spend time with a friend. To explain, even if it is not directly on account of this general practical consideration that he spends time with a friend, this general consideration (indicating what is or is not permissible) is all the same supposed to have some practical impact on whether he acts on his reason to spend time with his friend, which may be just that he enjoys the friend's company. (To consider another example, if Cullity's "attempts to justify the activity of writing [his] book" had proved unsuccessful, that presumably would for him have some impact on his future decisions to write such books.) As against this, Williams would want to say, I think, that to suggest that this more general consideration (about permissibility) should have this role in our practical deliberations is to have one thought too many. Otherwise put, this is to say that we should act – in the relevant cases – on reasons derived from our personal relationships and projects *simpliciter*: that general considerations about the (supposed) permissibility of such actions should not feature in our practical deliberations at all. The point here is, again, that reasons for acting derived from our personal relationships and projects do not in this general way stand in need of justification.

The point is a subtle one. Cullity thinks that the Extreme Demand is absurd, and so do I. Cullity can recognize that friendship involves acting out of a direct engagement with one's friend's welfare, and so do I. The difference between the position I am defending and Cullity's position concerns our differing arguments, *including the arguments we are prepared to entertain*, in reaching this conclusion. To explain, albeit roughly, while Cullity thinks the conclusion of the argument for Extreme Demand is absurd, he does not think *the challenge itself* is absurd; he would hardly have written the book he has if he thought that. But my point is that the challenge itself should be rejected; my argument is that it is a mistake to consider the very possibility that, say, friendship as we understand it and in the world as it is might be (in the light of the Extreme Demand) immoral. I say friendship "as we understand it" to flag two points: first, that as we understand friendship it does make significant demands on us, most obviously on our time (which could otherwise have been spent on relieving extreme poverty); but also, second, that as we understand friendship there are limits to the kinds of demands that friends might make on each other.[6] Granting those points, and so given the way in which we understand friendships and its demands, my point is that it is a mistake to consider whether friendship in this sense, and in the world as it is, might be morally wrong. To be prepared to consider *that*, to have that thought, is to have one thought too many, in the sense that Williams is highlighting.

To expand on my point above, my concern with Cullity's argument does not depend on any claim that he is defending a *purely* impartial conception of morality, for as I understand him he is not doing that. His position is more modestly that the Extreme Demand can be rejected from some "appropriately impartial point of view". So Cullity may argue that his strategy is just to show that in so far as some impartial moral theory seems to lead to the Extreme Demand it can be rejected by appeal to the impartial point of view itself; that is, that the argument from impartial morality to the Extreme Demand can be rejected *in its own terms*. But my point, again, is that we should not accept those terms, since to take up the challenge of showing how this argument from impartial morality fails in its own terms leads to us talking about personal relationships and projects as permissions.[7] And as I have argued, to think of our personal relationships and projects in *that* way is to fail to adequately recognize the nature and content of demands from personal relationships and projects. To be sure, Cullity's argument gives us a reason to reject the Extreme Demand but my point is that his argument gives us the wrong reason to reject it. I am happy to accept that the argument from impartial morality to the Extreme Demand fails in its own terms but that is not the reason I think we should reject it. Moreover that reason, as I say, provides us with one thought too many, thus obscuring the reason we should reject the Extreme Demand. What we need to reject here is the presumption implicit in impartial morality that our personal relationships and projects stand in need of justification.

Putting the point in the most favourable light, on the kind of view I have been describing, and taking issue with what one wants, is not just to pursue one's personal relationships and projects but to pursue them with a clear conscience, where conscience takes the form of some kind of impartial judge. That, for some, might seem only reasonable. It is certainly one way of understanding the place of morality in our lives. We need not on this view always be thinking about whether we are acting morally rightly. However, it remains true that everything we do falls within the scope of morality.[8] The question "But is this permissible?" may not in practice come up very often but the question is, all the same, always there to adjudicate if necessary. Williams's criticisms of what he calls the morality system are focused on morality as having *this* place in our lives, on its role as ultimate judge. It is this overweening of morality in our lives that Williams calls moralistic and his point is that we need not conceive of the moral or, as he would rather put it, the ethical in this way. So thinking of the claims that others make on us in this way, for example, is not morally (ethically) neutral.

One might object at this point, however, that it misrepresents impartial moral conscience, or even some appropriately impartial point of view, to say that it plays the role of some "ultimate judge". Of course in many cases we will act directly on reasons provided by a more partial point of view, and that, as I have conceded, is no challenge to Cullity. If asked "Why did you save that particular person rather than another?", Cullity might reasonably reply "It was my wife". Nevertheless, the impartial point of view, even as advanced by Cullity, is not just one point of view among others, which becomes clear when we consider the relationship between this point of view and more partial points of view. I have granted that Cullity's argument is just that the Extreme Demand can be rejected even from the impartial point of view. But why should we grant the impartial point of view that kind of authority, which is to say that kind of jurisdiction or scope, in our practical deliberations and lives?[9] And what follows for our personal relationships and projects if we do grant it that authority? We might put the point this way: even if we envisage both the impartial and partial points of view as providing us directly with reasons for action, where a potential conflict is suggested, even a modest impartialist like Cullity attempts to square the reasons derived from the partial point of view *with* the impartial point of view, as permissions, for example. The partial and impartial points of view are not, then, on the same footing here and the consequence of this is that the very source of certain partial reasons, our personal relationships and projects, can come to look problematic, since there is no question that the impartial point of view and the reasons derived from it need to be squared with *them*. In other words, such relationships and projects – not particular ones, of course, but the categories as sources of practical reasons – have no corner they can call their own and that the impartial point of view just has to accommodate itself to. It is in the nature of the impartial moral conscience that it can make no such accommodation; impartial moral conscience takes no prisoners.[10]

What Williams calls moralistic is, as I have noted, a certain conception of morality (or the ethical) that he has characterized by the term the "morality system". The way of understanding the place of morality in our lives that Williams associates with the morality system can be seen to lead, then, to a certain failure to appreciate or acknowledge the place of other values in our lives. Thus I have suggested, following Williams, that in our personal relationships with others the claims of morality here might seem to provide us with "one thought too many". So it might be thought that spending time with a friend is not a matter for my conscience at all, unless some very special context is provided.[11] This is not to deny that I might remain committed to a friend despite my moral questions here (say, about whether this is morally permissible) but to suggest that there is no place for such questions, that that kind of question discounts, to some extent, the value of friendship and its proper place in our lives. But it is important to be clear about the target of the argument here. To explain, the argument is not that we should reject *any* conception of impartialism as relevant to ethics. So, for example, impartiality understood simply as thinking that each of us is just one person among others is, I acknowledge, central to a conception of fairness that is itself an essential element in our moral thought. My objection is only to the way in which, on certain impartialist conceptions of ethics, we conceive of the conflict between certain moral and other values and then how that conflict is to be resolved. The view I am defending in this book, and that I began to outline explicitly in Chapter 2, is that certain values are themselves only revealed through the myriad, as I have called them, primitive ways in which we respond to other human beings in the course of living a complete human life. So to take the case of friendship, my objection to impartialist ethics is to theories that suppose that the values that are internal to friendship, and that may seem to conflict with the demands of impartial morality, can themselves be adequately characterized or captured independently of the pattern of responses between friends through which those values are revealed. When I say that such impartialism discounts the values internal to friendship, what I mean is that, in so far as we see having such relationships as subject to the findings of some impartial point of view – as when we ask, for example, "Is friendship permissible in this world?" – we undermine that pattern of responsiveness between friends that is internal to recognizing the values that friendship involves and the place such values occupy in a complete human life.

## Moral and other values

To expand on the above thoughts, we can see the same kind of discounting and undermining in connection to other aspects of human life as well. In a related discussion by Cora Diamond about the potential conflict between morality and other values, she considers the case of humour:

> No better example can be found of an element of human nature capable of clashing with morality … than our sense of what is funny. Jokes, especially vulgar ones, depend heavily on stereotypes and on topics taken to be intrinsically funny, like sex and drunkenness; they thus have enormous potential for moral offensiveness, and are frequently cruel … But how far should the jokey side of us, what Orwell called the Sancho Panza in us, be squashed into the space which morality (conceived in this or that particular way) is willing to allow it? … If some answers to such a question are felt to be puritanical or moralistic, that feeling is (I am suggesting) not primarily a response to the content of the answer but rather to how the question itself is conceptualized – to the underlying ideas about human life and human good. Under cover, as it were, of "authority of Morality", something with its own rights is being denied them.                                    (1997: 215)

The problem here is with accommodating the notion that there might be some area of human life "with its own rights". For the underlying thought is that, unless some very special context is provided, in this area of human life morality just does not have a say, hence it has no business causing us unease. I mean of course *real* moral unease, for, as Diamond also notes, we sometimes say of some potentially offensive joke, "That is not funny", when it quite patently *is* funny and we cannot stop ourselves from laughing. The point is that once morality is allowed the kind of adjudicating role I have been discussing it may be difficult to really appreciate much that is humanly valuable, including many things that are funny. Mercifully, in this sort of case where the moral stakes are pretty low, moral worries usually lose out to the kinds of spontaneous impulse and tendencies to which humour appeals – but not always.

I have already mentioned in Chapter 2 the ludicrous obscenity trial of Max Harris, the hapless editor of *Angry Penguins*, over his publication of the fabricated Australian poet Ern Malley. As I noted there, Heyward in his account of the trial suggests that the testimony of the arresting officer, Vogelesang, "brought the house down". While the gallery clearly saw the humour in the situation, the police and prosecution were deadly serious. One might like to think that such puritanical tendencies lie in the past but sadly it is not so. We are perhaps less priggish than Vogelesang and the prosecution but many still take umbrage at, and seek to censor, humour involving sex and lewdness. For a more recent example, consider Monty Python's last film, *The Meaning of Life*. Quite a few scenes in this film cross some moral line for some; it was originally banned in Ireland.[12] One morally questionable scene presents a condemned criminal allowed to choose the manner of his own death. In the scene, Graham Chapman's character, Arthur Jarrett, is chased off a cliff by about a dozen almost naked women wearing crash helmets for the offence of "first-degree making of gratuitous sexist jokes in a moving picture". This scene will no doubt offend some people, but it is very funny.

The problem with humour is, in a way, starker than the kind of worry presented by personal relationships and projects. In the case of jokes, unlike personal relationships and projects, the very features that make them funny are often also the features that cause moral offence. Hence if we are going to allow morality a look-in here much of the richness of comedy risks being lost. By comparison, moral oversight of our personal relationships and projects need not be directly destructive of them. Nevertheless, the idea that morality has this kind of adjudicating role in one's life does make a difference to how one conceives of the values internal to personal relationships and projects and of the demands that they make on one. I need not, in writing philosophy books or spending time with friends and loved ones, always, or even very often, be questioning whether it is permissible for me to live this way. For example, I may be confident, even if I cannot fully articulate my reasons, that all this is permissible. But, and this is a different point, *I may otherwise resent the question,* as it seems to me that my friends and loved ones might resent me were I to ask it. Such resentment shows the place and authority of personal relationships and projects in our lives, yet it cannot help but offend against morality's adjudicating role, for morality so understood cannot countenance the thought that there is any area of human life in which *that* role does not apply.

However, one might argue that the example of humour shows that morality actually does have the kind of adjudicating role in our practical deliberations that I am denying. So it may be argued that the contrast between morality and humour has not yet been pushed far enough, pushed as we might say to the limit: that some examples of humour are so morally repellent that we genuinely believe we ought not to laugh at them. Doesn't this show that morality does after all occupy a special place in our practical deliberations? And if that is so, doesn't it support the idea that where a conflict occurs between moral and other values, that conflict must be resolved in accordance with demands of some (perhaps impartial) moral conscience? I am not denying that there will be conflicts between what Diamond calls the jokey side of us and morality. My point is again only about the way in which we conceive of this conflict. In some cases a joke will be morally objectionable but very funny and it will be natural to say that morality should give way. In other cases the situation will be the reverse. For example, in the case of an extremely morally offensive joke told in a context where it will cause real distress or harm, we may conclude that the joke is a joke too far. The crucial point is just that each side, the jokey side of us and morality, has its own rights and that morality has no special authority to adjudicate where they conflict. If we do decide that a given joke goes too far, that will not be because morality plays an adjudicating role in the conflict between humour and morality here, but because of the way in which we conceive through our responses and subsequent judgement on this occasion of the relevant limits of their domains. What I am objecting to is only the idea that morality has some special authority to judge other areas of our life and the values internal to them.

Even in cases where humour may be seen as extremely morally offensive, one might question whether it is really true that we ought not to laugh, whether it is appropriate to raise moral objections. To illustrate the point, consider another kind of moralism; the thesis in aesthetics that moral defects in a work of art may also be aesthetic defects. Perhaps the most subtle exponent of this view is Noël Carroll, who defends a thesis he calls "moderate moralism", according to which "in some instances a moral defect in an artwork can be an aesthetic defect, [while] sometimes a moral virtue can count as an aesthetic virtue" (1998: 419). Carroll's own example in support of this thesis is apposite to my discussion of humour since it concerns a work of satire, specifically Bret Easton Ellis's novel *American Psycho*. Carroll's point is to argue that this work is really a failed satire. As Carroll has it:

> The author intended it as a satire of the rapacious eighties in the USA. He presented a serial killer as a symbol of the vaunted securities marketeer of Reaganomics. However, the serial killings depicted in the novel are so graphically brutal that readers are not able morally to get past the gore in order to savour the parody. (1996: 232)

According to Carroll, Ellis's "moral understanding of the possible moral significance of murders, such as the ones he depicted, was flawed, and he was condemned for promoting it" (*ibid.*). But in so far as his novel fails to illicit the right emotional uptake from its audience, the book is also an aesthetic failure. Thus the moral flaw in the work was also an aesthetic flaw. Central to Carroll's argument – and relevant to mine – is the idea that a "morally sensitive audience" will condemn Ellis for the violence and thus fail to appreciate the satire. As Carroll says, a "work is flawed if it contains a failure in moral perspective that a morally sensitive audience could detect, such that that discovery would compromise the effect of the work on its own terms" (*ibid.*: 234). Crucial here is the claim about what a morally sensitive audience *could* detect, since Carroll's point is that "even where given audiences do not detect the moral flaws ... the artwork may still be aesthetically flawed, since in those cases the moral flaws sit like time-bombs ready to explode aesthetically once morally sensitive viewers, listeners and readers encounter them" (*ibid.*). Here one might think Carroll has pushed his point rather too far; what is decisive in assessing a work of art now is not how you or I or (more generally) ordinarily morally decent people respond to it, but how some ideally morally sensitive audience might respond to it. But why should the point of view of such an audience be the correct point of view for assessing a work of art? As Peter Lamarque has suggested:

> by introducing the idea of a "morally sensitive audience" Carroll makes the question of response normative. The suggestion seems to be that the right kind of audience *ought* not to pursue the uptake invited. … [But] [m]ight not the "right" audience be less one that is morally sensitive, more one that is sensitive to *literature*? It would beg the question to presume that the ideal reader of literature, the one best able to recognize literary value, must have a heightened moral sensibility. Perhaps the ideal reader … is someone able to set aside his or her own moral beliefs to enter the world of the work, someone who is not morally squeamish. (2009: 289)

The above discussion illustrates again the tendency of morality to overween in our lives. Further, what the above example makes plain is that it is not the content of morality that is at issue here but how we conceptualize the conflict between moral and other values, including literary values. So, while I have focused on impartialist theories of ethics, the potential for morality to overween in our lives exists wherever the moral point of view is *necessarily* taken to be the point of view *from which* to resolve the conflict between moral and other values.[13] Certainly, if one reads *American Psycho*, say, from the perspective of morality, as we might, then one may not be amused. But it is not at all obvious that that is a failure of the work so much as one's own failure to, as Lamarque says, "set aside" one's own moral beliefs.[14] To be clear, the idea here is that to appreciate the satire, our moral beliefs are not outweighed but in some way bracketed. Once raised, of course, such beliefs may detract from the satire, but that, we might think, *is a good reason not to raise them.* But to think that is to deny morality the kind of adjudicating role in our lives that I have been objecting to. Conversely, to grant this role to morality is to deny the independent authority of other values, including aesthetic values: in the present example, to suggest, in effect, that we can decide in advance and on certain moral grounds the limits of satire. But who knows what an audience sensitive to *both* moral and literary values will be able to savour?

One may be inclined to believe that there must be some kind of relation between moral and aesthetic value; indeed, given what I have said about the role of certain primitive responses in moral thought and understanding, I think Carroll has a point at least about how actual audiences, with their particular moral and aesthetic sensibilities, are capable of responding to particular works of art. But it is quite another thing to think it appropriate to judge a work of art from the point of view of morality. That this is not the point of view from which to assess a work of art is perhaps evident in some recent *reappraisals* of *American Psycho*. For as Lamarque also notes, now that the initial moral furore surrounding it has abated, some critics have been much more willing to see it as a successful satire.[15] Hence we might question whether in our assessment of an artwork – or even a joke – the perspective of morality should have the kind of authority that Carroll suggests. In summary, while in an obvious sense moral concerns *could* be raised in a case like *American Psycho*, it is not clear that they ought to be raised, or that people sensitive to a broader conception of the human good will in fact raise them.

## The challenge of world poverty

To return to what are perhaps more central moral concerns, I am not denying that other human beings, including those suffering extreme poverty and deprivation, make moral demands on us, nor denying even that we should be doing more than we are currently to help those in desperate need. My point is only about the way in which we conceive of those demands, which in turn depends on the way in which we conceive of morality and its place in our lives. And, as I have argued, we should not take it as open for morality to question *in a general way* the place and authority of personal relationships and projects in our lives. So when I say we should be doing more to help the world's most needy I take it for granted that we could be doing more without our commitment to our personal relationships and projects even coming into question.

At this point I do want to say something more positive about how we should envisage our moral relations with the world's desperately poor, and here I part company with Williams. Indeed, it seems to me that while Williams acknowledges the challenge of world poverty, he is disappointingly silent about how we are to meet it.[16] Moreover, it strikes me as a feature of Williams's ethical writing that his attacks on ethical theorizing leaves it quite unclear how one might meet the challenge of global justice. As Martha Nussbaum has pointed out in this connection, a puzzling question for Williams's ethical writings "concerns the relationship between the ethical and the political". As she goes on to say:

> Williams later maintained that his attack on ethical theorizing left intact the aspiration to construct *political* theories, which might be valuable guides. But where does this leave those among the great Western political theorists such as Aristotle, Cicero, Rousseau, Kant, and John Rawls, who put a moral theory at the core of their political theories? Williams singles out Rawls as an example of the criticized class of moral theories; and yet his later statement suggests that after all he might admit the usefulness of Rawls's theory, given its political nature. In any case the source of the distinction between an acceptable aspiration to a theory of political justice and an unacceptable aspiration to a theory of individual morality is left obscure. Williams's general failure to engage systematically with Rawls's ideas about social and political justice leaves important issues unresolved.                (Nussbaum 2003: 6)

Many people, me included, will take Williams's failure to engage systematically with ideas about social and political justice as a gap, if not a shortcoming, in his ethical writings. Nussbaum explains this in Williams's case by reference to his "Nietzschean pessimism and irrationalism" (*ibid.*), and there may be some truth in this. In any case, one might have hoped, thinking about poverty and the extreme injustice that this undoubtedly involves, that Williams would have something more positive or constructive to say about how we might meet the challenge of world poverty.

To turn to my own more positive thoughts concerning our moral relations to the world's desperately poor, one obvious way in which the world's desperately poor may be an object of our moral concern is by being the object of our sympathy. That might not seem very encouraging; human beings, as we all know, have limited sympathies. Moreover, one might say that a powerful part of the attraction of the impartial moral point of view is that it provides us with reasons for acting out of concern for the interests of others even when we are not sympathetically disposed to do so. Nevertheless, if, as I have argued, the impartial moral point of view seriously discounts or distorts our understanding of important human values, then one way of meeting the challenge of world poverty may be to examine the ways in which our natural sympathies for other human beings might be extended. A lot may depend on how we understand sympathy. As I suggested in Chapter 2, and have argued more extensively elsewhere (see esp. Taylor 2002), we should think of sympathy not as mere feeling or sentiment, but as a kind of primitive responsiveness to other human beings. Such sympathetic responses, I have suggested, involve, first, being moved by the suffering of another immediately and without thinking. But further, and second, I have argued that our sympathetic responses to others also help found our sense of what it is to be human in the sense that it is only through such responsiveness to others that we conceive of others as the kinds of beings capable of making certain claims on us at all.

I shall not expand my previous arguments to the above claims here. My point is just that if one takes sympathy to play this kind of constitutive role in our conception of morality, then we will understand the claims that others make on us very differently than they are understood in impartialist moral theories. One way of spelling that out is to say that in understanding the moral claims another might make on me what is most basic is my relationship to the other, and that *immediacy* – such as when another is suffering right in front of me – indicates the most basic kind of moral relationship two human beings might have to each other.[17] It is, we might say, in the context of this kind of immediacy that our sympathetic responses to (and relationship with) others first emerge. Thus, we might also argue, we understand the claims made on us by those far away as *extensions of*, not as *analogous to*, this kind of relationship. To put the point another way, what is important, perhaps, is that we understand the claims of those far away in terms of the extension of our existing web of relationships with other human beings not by picking out some common factor in both cases, such as the good I could do for another. But this kind of "picking out" of a common factor is just what impartialism urges on us.

In focusing on my relationship to another, the impartialist may complain, as Cullity puts it, that I "make the reason to help other people too self-regarding" in that "this offers a fact about *me* as the reason for helping, rather than the good it would do for *him*" (2004: 22). So, as Cullity goes on to say, "there does seem to be a big difference between taking as your reason for this aim the benefit to them, and taking as your reason the relation between them and you" (*ibid.*). But I think such an objection as applied to me would be misplaced. There is indeed a difference here, but if morality, as I would contend, is founded in part on the (sympathetic) way one particular human being, myself, say, may respond to another particular human being, then there will be nothing objectionably self-regarding at least in the thought that the relation between them and me *provides* my reason for helping them. To be clear, the relation between them and me is not itself my reason for helping them. On the contrary, and as I alluded to in Chapter 2, my sympathetic responses to others (including remote strangers) itself helps to constitute the web of human relationships through which we recognize another as an appropriate object of various kinds of concern. Thus, it is in virtue of such relationships and such a conception of another that we have so much as the idea that they provide us with certain moral reasons for action. But that is not the same thing as saying that my relationship with another is itself my reason for providing them with aid.

## Conclusion

In this chapter I have focused not on the way particular instances of moral reflection and judgement may be distorted in ways that may be characterized as moralistic, but on the idea that particular ethical theories or approaches may themselves be moralistic in the specific sense that such theories and approaches lead to morality overweening in our lives. I have indicated how such theories and approaches are not simply too demanding but involve morality, as we might now say, trespassing into others areas of human life where they have no authority to adjudicate or even where moral judgement is out of place. One might question whether this kind of overweening is a necessary feature of the impartialist theories that I, following Williams, have targeted.[18] Then there is the further question about whether some kind of Aristotelian virtue ethical theory might be able to meet the kind of objection I have raised. On the first question, part of the reason I have discussed Cullity's response to the Extreme Demand is to show how the problem of overweening is not so much connected to the content of any particular theory but about how we conceive of moral thought and judgement and its place in our practical deliberations and lives more generally. On the second question, I can only make two brief comments here. The first is that, at least with some prominent theories of virtue ethics, the overweening problem will still come up simply because what makes for human excellence, or virtue, on such theories can conflict badly with the demands of personal relationships. So it has always struck me, for example, although I cannot argue the point here, that while Aristotle assigns a central place to friendship in the good or flourishing life for man, what seems ruled out on his account is the idea that friendship and other personal relationships may require us to act in ways that to some extent undermine our own flourishing. The second point, which is really a qualification of the first, is just to note that the classification "Aristotelian virtue ethical theories" covers a multitude of specific theories that draw on or are inspired by Aristotle's ethics in very different ways, and so to concede that it may be that some such theories are not liable to the arguments raised in this chapter.

It is of course controversial to call the theories and approaches I have discussed here moralistic in the sense that they lead to a distortion of moral reflection and judgement. To be clear, in claiming this I am not suggesting that the impartial moral theorists I have targeted are necessarily moralizers in the sense I have considered earlier in the book. Further, as I have noted, the impartialist thought that morally we are, all of us, in some sense just one person among others is an important moral thought and one that I certainly do not want to dismiss. My point is just that the structure of moral thought and judgement that impartialist moral thinking may further impose leads to morality overweening in our lives, just to note one way in which impartialism in ethics, and even broadly construed, might lead us astray. All the same it will be argued by many that morality has precisely the kind of adjudicating role in our lives that such theories and approaches lead to and which I have criticized. So on that view it will seem simply question-begging to say that morality so construed plays an "overweening" role in our lives.

At this point we return again to question I introduced in Chapter 2 of how we should understand the nature of moral thought or reflection and judgement and indeed how moral reflection is related to making moral judgements. I shall return specifically to address this question in the next two chapters. In the next chapter I shall argue in somewhat more detail that we need to understand moral thought or reflection much more broadly than many moral theorists currently allow, and specifically – as I have touched on in Chapter 2 – that there are modes of moral thought or reflection that extend beyond simply making moral judgements as that is commonly understood. In Chapter 6 I shall argue further that the broader conception of moral thought that I have outlined suggests a very different conception of moral judgement than most moral theories, and certainly impartialist moral theories, can allow: specifically, that there is more than one conception of the moral life so that moral judgements are not always universalizable. This argument poses a direct challenge to impartial morality as I have characterized it in this chapter and spells out in somewhat more detail reasons for rejecting it.

# FIVE

# Moral judgement and moral reflection

In the previous chapter I considered a kind of moralism as the over-weening of morality and, in response to this, what the proper scope or limits to moral thought and judgement might be. More explicitly, I suggested that the way in which certain moral theories (and particularly impartialist theories) conceive of the conflict between moral and other values distorts our understanding of important human values; in particular by undermining the kind of responsiveness to others through which such values are revealed. In this respect then, as I shall argue in this chapter, the kind of overweening of morality that I considered in the previous chapter rests on an inadequate conception of moral thought quite generally. More specifically, I shall argue that moralism involves a too narrow conception of moral thought, one in which moral thought is ultimately about making moral judgements. As I argued in Chapter 2, one thing that may be lacking in our judgements of another is scope for a kind of pity, a response through which we might recognize the humanity of those we would judge. Such responsiveness indicates an important dimension to moral thought that the moralizer may miss. My focus in Chapter 2 was on how particular moral judgements may be distorted by a lack of such responsiveness to those we would judge. But one need not be a moralizer in the sense I examined there to have the kind of overly narrow view of moral thought that concerns me. So, a prevalent view in much moral theorizing, at least in analytic philosophy, is precisely that moral thought *is* ultimately about making moral judgements in just the way I am challenging. What I shall argue in more detail in this chapter is how the kind of responsiveness I touched on in Chapter 2 may indicate further modes of moral thought or reflection, apart from making moral judgements as we normally understand that, and in so doing reveal how prevailing conceptions of moral thought are deficient. This is not to say that defenders of such conceptions lack the kinds of responsiveness that I highlighted in Chapter 2 but to suggest that they discount its importance in moral thought quite generally.

The idea that there may be modes of moral thought apart from those directly leading to, or expressed in, moral judgements, although a challenge to what might be called the prevailing view of moral thought, is not entirely new. In different ways a number of philosophers, including Iris Murdoch ([1970] 1985), Martha Nussbaum (1990), Cora Diamond (1991), Raimond Gaita (1991) and, most recently and explicitly, Alice Crary (2007) have argued that moral thought may involve more than simply making moral judgements.[1] In order to get clear how that might be though, we need to specify what exactly is being contrasted here, for one way to understand moral judgement, as Crary notes, is as "any episode of moral thought whatsoever" (*ibid.*: 10 n.). This is not, as I have already touched on, how I have understood making moral judgements. On the contrary, and following Crary, I understand moral judgement somewhat more narrowly to involve the application of moral concepts – both so-called "thin" moral concepts such as "right" and "wrong" and "thick" concepts such as "courageous" or "cowardly"[2] – to people, actions and events. The result of such application, as I noted in Chapter 1, is that we should be able to assert a particular proposition, for example, "He was wrong to cheat on his wife" or "It was cowardly for him to lie about his infidelity". Such propositions, we might say, are the content of our moral judgements on such occasions.

So how might moral thought extend beyond moral judgement so defined? Consider again the kind of example I gave in Chapter 2. To respond in one's judgement of another with pity requires attributes, in particular emotional capacities of response, quite apart from the application of moral concepts, principles or theories to particular situations. But this is not the only way participation in the moral life extends farther than the making of moral judgements. Beyond this there may be situations that call for a kind of moral responsiveness to another where there is no place for making a moral judgement. This is not to say, in another way, that in such situations we will not be called on to exercise moral thought and understanding: of course we are so required. But talk in this connection about moral thought and understanding need not refer to our ability to make moral judgements or to the practice of making moral judgements at all. Rather, the exercise or moral thought and understanding at issue may involve modes of responsiveness to others that we may nevertheless identify as genuine aspects of our moral sensibility.

To illustrate, consider an example that clearly does involve the making of moral judgements. Suppose, in the context of a philosophy tutorial, there is a discussion about whether and under what conditions abortion should be morally permissible. We can imagine various members of this tutorial group advancing moral judgements and then defending them by reference to certain moral principles or ultimately moral theories. At the same time it may be that a member of this tutorial is becoming extremely distressed about this whole discussion. What this situation calls for, we might think, is not the making of another moral judgement, although it certainly requires the exercise of our moral sensibility in some sense; it requires a certain capacity on the part of the tutor to respond in morally appropriate ways. And we may hope that the tutor has the moral sensibility required here: the kind of sensibility that might lead him, say, to divert the conversation to some other topic for discussion,[3] although nothing in current philosophical training – or, in my experience at least, in current university teaching training – will have helped him to acquire or exercise such a sensibility.[4]

It may be objected that here too what is required is a particular moral judgement; that in the circumstances and in the light, say, of certain moral concepts (such as compassion or kindness) the tutor should reach the judgement that this particular line of discussion should now end. But two points here: first, this objection takes it that the student's distress is in an important sense open to view, specifically that it does not require a certain developed moral sensibility, involving a certain responsiveness to others, to recognize that the student is distressed. In so far as recognizing that the student is distressed involves thought itself dependent on, or simply engaging, such responsiveness, it is moral thought that is to be distinguished from any judgement the tutor might make on account of the insight such thought provides. It is not itself a part of making a moral judgement.

Second, one might progress so far as to recognize that this student is distressed and that one ought to do something about the situation but nevertheless fail to act; as it may be if the tutor, imagining that the student is about to break into tears, were to panic or lose their nerve so that they, as we might say, "freeze up". We might say in such a case that the tutor does not know exactly what to do. All the same, their failure here is not merely or primarily a failure of knowledge so much as a kind of practical infirmity. To explain, what one needs beyond the knowledge that the student is distressed is the capacity to respond effectively. But in dealing effectively with a situation like this our response may in fact be – even need to be – quite immediate. In such a case, like the kind of situation I considered in Chapter 2 with pitying Dimmesdale, it is not as if we make the decision to respond in this way rather than that; we just act immediately, in a certain sense, without thinking further at all. That is, our response here might be what I have called a primitive response to another. But to call such responses primitive, to say that we may respond in such situations immediately or without thinking, is not to say, as I have argued, that such responses are *thoughtless*. Being thoughtful here – beyond having the thought "This student is distressed" – is of a piece with having the kind of developed moral sensibility alluded to above; it is something that is expressed or shows itself in one's mode and extent of responsiveness to others.[5]

I have suggested that moral thought may involve, beyond making moral judgements, responding to another in the kind of immediate or primitive ways I have suggested above. But this is not to say that moral thought is restricted to responding in the kind of immediate ways I have outlined. So I do not want to deny what I think is in fact also very important: that such responsiveness to others may invite *further* moral thought or reflection of a more extended and self-conscious kind on, say, aspects of the life and experience of another. And this further moral thought or reflection too need not be directed at making a moral judgement about how to act. Rather, it may be that the point of such thought or reflection is simply to see another person's character more clearly. Thus moral thought may involve the kind of "careful and just *attention*" that Murdoch speaks of when she describes how a woman, M, "an intelligent and well-intentioned person", is able to overcome through introspection her prejudice against her daughter in law, D, who she feels is beneath he son ([1970] 1985: 17). As Murdoch says, M may "tell herself: 'I am old-fashioned and conventional. I may be prejudiced and narrow-minded. I may be snobbish. I am certainly jealous. Let me look again'" (*ibid.*). Such thought is, I concede, not immediate in the sense that I have outlined, although it does depend, as I want to argue, on much thought about other human beings that is given through the kind of primitive responsiveness I have been discussing.

I have a special reason though for focusing on our immediate responses to others, and it is useful to briefly discuss here Murdoch's example of M and D. As Murdoch herself concedes, it may be difficult to determine M's motives in thinking again about D. As she says, "Some people might say 'she deludes herself' [because she doesn't want to think of her son as unfortunate] while others would say she is moved by love or justice [to see D more clearly]" (*ibid.*: 18). There is, that is to say, a danger of self-deception in the kind of self-conscious reflection that Murdoch is discussing. And now one of the reasons I shall focus on our immediate responses to those around us is to argue, as will become clear below, that it may be through attending to our immediate responses to other people, but also crucially the *lack* of certain immediate responses, that we might get a better understanding of our own motivations, and more generally our own character and its limitations, and thus guard against self-deception in our more self-conscious moral reflections. Thus my argument in this chapter is in important respects continuous with the discussion of Chapter 3 concerning our immediate responses to certain supposedly morally problematic works of art.

But to return to the main argument, as far as morality is concerned what is demanded of us is not merely the capacity to make moral judgements but also certain capacities of response: the capacity to respond to people and events in ways that, considering my first point above, show our understanding of others and of the situation we find ourselves in and, considering my second point, involve effective agency. All this is not, as I say, the kind of understanding that is acquired simply by learning moral concepts, principles and theories and being able to apply them in moral judgement or deploy them in argument. In so far as the capacities of response that are required of us are *emotional* capacities, we can say that understanding here, at least in part, is a matter of feeling. However the responses that are required of us here are not merely emotional responses but include, as I say, immediate, yet still highly purposive or thoughtful, actions performed towards others, including, for example, coming to another's aid. The moral significance of these responses, quite apart from our moral judgements, including judgements about others, is something that we tend, quite unreasonably I suggest, to discount. One reason that we might discount them is because one thinks that, contrary to what I am claiming, they do not involve moral thought at all and so are not morally significant.

By way of a start on addressing this objection, consider an obvious kind of example of the kind of responses in question. A child has fallen off a crowded pier and is drowning. In this kind of case, and given that I can swim, the very judgement "The child is drowning, I ought to help" seems out of place. This is not to say that there is no judgement that someone not involved in this event, or that I after the fact, might make here. Rather, it is to point out that what is required of me here and now is not a judgement but an action, one that should be immediately forthcoming. However, there are two points about such an action that we need to note. First, all too often such an action, although relatively easy to perform, will *not* be forthcoming; there are many stories of people – seemingly decent people – failing to come to the aid of others even when that involves little cost to them.[6] Second, where such an action is forthcoming – and partly because of my first point – there is something impressive about it; indeed, we are apt to say that it displays certain presence of mind in anyone who is thus moved. Such a response, although quite immediate, displays a particular kind, or quality, of thought; we might call it a kind of engagement with people and events around the agent. Such a case shows that what morality requires of us – and what is all the same more than we can count on – is the kind of immediate yet purposive responsiveness to others I indicated in the example of the tutor above, the kind of responsiveness that is displayed here in immediately coming to this child's aid.

## Moral thought and literature

I have pointed to some of the ways in which moral thought may involve more than making, and defending, moral judgements. But what, in more detail, is really involved in such thought? One place, although not the only place, to look for such thought or reflection, as noted by the philosophers I have mentioned earlier, is literature, both in certain literary works and in our responses to them. For while literature is rarely concerned with the presenting and defending of moral judgements, principles or theories it does at least sometimes have, as one of its specific aims, the aim to enlarge our moral sensibilities.

I take it then that the role of literature in connection with moral thought is not simply to provide good examples. Almost anyone would accept that in helping a person to understand some (perhaps difficult) moral problem or concept it may be useful to give them certain examples of a literary kind. But to claim that the role of literature is exhausted by its role in providing a pool of such examples suggests that once the relevant moral problem or concept is understood the literary example itself is superfluous and can be dispensed with. Of course against this it has been argued by a number of philosophers, including those I have noted above, that *the ways in which* literature (although not necessarily just literature[7]) illuminates important human values are essential to any adequate understanding of those values. There is a distinct divide, at least in the case of philosophers broadly in the analytic tradition, between two conceptions of moral thought and reflection, a divide that is illustrated by a now well-known exchange between Diamond and Onora O'Neill. Since that debate goes some way to explaining how, I shall argue, we should understand the role of literature in moral thought and reflection, it is useful to outline their respective visions of moral thought and reflection *per se*.

The above-mentioned exchange was motivated by O'Neill's (1980) review of Stephen Clark's book *The Moral Status of Animals*. What O'Neill finds wanting in Clark's book are arguments in favour of his claims about the moral status of animals. Where what is needed are arguments in defence of the moral status of animals O'Neill finds only appeals to the heart, appeals that, first, are unlikely to convince anyone whose heart does not already so incline them and, second, are, in so far as they are appeals to the heart, not a legitimate exercise of moral thought or reflection at all but rather simply assertion. Against this, Diamond argues that between mere assertion and argument (in O'Neill's sense) there lie other varieties of moral thought that O'Neill appears blind to. Specifically, Diamond argues that moral thought quite properly involves the exercise of certain capacities of emotional response as well. Further, while acknowledging that our responses to literature (or to the world) may be initially wholly unreflective – as it is she says, for example, when we respond in "delighted amazement and wonder at fairy tales" – Diamond goes on to argue that, through the development of these capacities, we may come to a:

> deeper understanding and an enriching of our own thought and experience; we can come to have a sense of what is alive, and what is shallow, sentimental, cheap; as we make comparisons, we come to know what are the reasons for our interest in this, our feeling that that is important.  (Diamond 1991: 303)

All this Diamond describes as "a kind of learning to think; it plays an essential role in the education of the emotions and in the development of moral sensibility" (*ibid.*). While Diamond is not denying the importance of the kind of critical attention invited by philosophical argument, to this she wants to add that "critical attention to the character and quality of thought in a work may be asked of a reader in many other ways as well" (*ibid.*). So, just as a work may be unconvincing because it is internally inconsistent, a work may be unconvincing, may fail, as we might say, to ring true, simply because the thought in it is shallow or sentimental. Indeed, to put the shoe, as it were, on the other foot, while a work, say, of moral philosophy may meet the highest standards of philosophical argument, the character and quality of the thought in that work might, in light of other kinds of critical attention that Diamond is highlighting, be found wanting in various ways, might itself appear shallow, for example.

To see what, for Diamond, is involved in moral thought, consider her discussion of Wordsworth's *Lyrical Ballads*, an example, she thinks, that indicates the way in which our capacities for emotional response are essentially involved in moral thought leading to being convinced of morally significant truths. First, as Diamond notes, some of these poems are "clearly meant to lead their audience to new moral responses" (*ibid.*: 297); indeed, as Diamond goes on to say, Wordsworth indicates in his preface his intention "to enlarge the reader's moral and emotional sensibilities" (*ibid.*). Second, as Diamond goes on to argue, an expression of the view of human nature conveyed in Wordsworth's poems:

> may be found in "The Old Cumberland Beggar," when the response of the villagers to the beggar is explained: we have all of us one human heart. But what is it to be convinced of that? What *sort* of conviction is it that such poems aim at? It cannot be separated from an understanding of oneself, from an acknowledgment of certain capacities of response in oneself as appropriate both to their object and to one's own nature.
>
> (*Ibid.*: 298)

Diamond finds the example of the "The Old Cumberland Beggar" particularly interesting "because the moral aim is very clear, and because there is actually an argument … in it" (*ibid.*: 297). Her point is though that while Wordsworth is certainly trying to convince us of something, it is not the argument we might abstract from his work that does the convincing.

Learning to think in moral ways then, we might say, is not simply a matter of learning to judge: learning to apply specific moral concepts correctly to people and actions in specific situations. The point is not simply that the range of moral concepts is too narrow to account for the kind of thought that Diamond envisages. I grant that perhaps morality may include concepts such as "shallow" or "sentimental", that we might then apply in moral judgement, for example when we judge that an argument is shallow. But, again, *recognizing* that something is shallow, being able to make the kinds of distinctions that Diamond is concerned with, is not itself a matter of simply applying moral concepts to people or their actions; it requires beyond that the kind of responses Diamond has highlighted, responses that are not thought of as appropriate because of some *independent conception* of their object since the moral ideas that get expressed through such responses cannot be separated, as she says, from an acknowledgement of these "capacities of response … as appropriate both to their object and to one's own nature". Although someone might now ask: what is the significance of this kind of responsiveness and the thought involved in it? Morality is, after all, a practical matter. So someone might object that moral reasons are practical reasons and moral thought should end or result in action not mere contemplation.

Against the above objection one might reasonably reply that the kind of "careful and just *attention*" to others that I noted that Murdoch speaks of is itself an important moral achievement. But leaving that point aside, part of my reply to this objection is to point out again how moral agency may include certain primitive responses to people and events, responses that help constitute a background of moral thought or reflection but which are not themselves mediated by specific thoughts. The tutor in my example above, I have suggested, may respond to the distressed student immediately, which is to say without deliberation *and* intelligently. But another part of my reply is to consider the way in which a person's moral thought shows itself not in the specific judgements they make, but in how they live their life as a whole, including all those responses and patterns of response to others or to the world generally that go to characterizing a particular life. In examining the character of a particular life we are examining all that a person says and does and what that shows about the quality of that person's moral thought as a whole. One possibility is that a person may have mastered all the important moral concepts and arrive at all the right moral judgements, yet find their life is a moral failure because – what goes beyond this – at crucial points when certain capacities of response were required of them they were found wanting. An inability to respond appropriately to the specific demands of certain situations has, I shall argue, practical import beyond the capacity in any given situation to make the correct moral judgement. In order to show that, I need to look at a specific example and, unsurprisingly given what I have just said, it comes from literature.

## Lord Jim

An example that, first, brings home to us how morally significant are the kinds of primitive responses I have indicated above, and second, and related to this, something of what serious moral thought or reflection requires of us apart from a capacity to make the correct moral judgement, is Conrad's novel *Lord Jim* ([1900] 2007). This novel tells the story of Jim, a young English officer in the Merchant Service, a man who dreams of being a hero – who even expects it – and is only waiting for his opportunity, yet who, when the time comes, fails shamefully to live up to his vision of himself.

The fateful incident occurs when he is first mate on the merchant ship the *Patna*, delivering eight hundred Muslim pilgrims to their Holy Land. The journey has been uneventful, the sea calm, "smooth and cool to the eye like a sheet of ice" (*ibid.*: 15), when the *Patna* strikes something just below the surface. The collision is barely noticeable but the outer hull is breached and water rushes in, filling up to the forward bulkhead. With the *Patna* hardly seaworthy and with nothing but the heavily corroded bulkhead (bits of it came off in Jim's hand) between the inrushing sea and the sleeping pilgrims, Jim imagines that catastrophe is inevitable, that the ship will sink at any moment. Yet Jim is unable to act; so vivid is his imagination, so clearly can he see the impending disaster, that he stands, horrified, rooted to a spot on deck while the other white crew members, captain included, disgrace themselves by trying to release one of the lifeboats, so saving themselves while leaving their charges to a terrible death. Jim is disgusted by their cowardice and refuses to help them. But the next moment he has himself jumped over the side and into their boat. As it turns out, however, the *Patna* does not sink, being saved and towed to safety by another ship, and Jim is called to answer for his act of cowardice before a court of inquiry, which punishes him by cancelling his certificate and thus his occupation.

Jim's story is told in three ways as the book progresses: first, in the third person by an omniscient narrator up to the point where Jim faces the court of inquiry; then as related by Marlow, the narrator in several of Conrad's novels, in a long (very long) talk to a group of people after dinner, in which Marlow tells of his experience and impressions of Jim from first meeting him at the inquiry; and finally, in the form of a letter by Marlow to one of those present at that dinner and relating events of Jim's life after Marlow saw him for the last time. Looked at another way, *Lord Jim* divides into two distinct parts: the first dealing with events on the *Patna* and the second dealing with Jim's time in the remote settlement of Patusan, where he retreats from the world to very quickly become its virtual absolute ruler.

Central to the narrative though, what holds the story together is Marlow's sympathy for, and interest in, Jim. While Jim's crime, as Marlow sees it, is so serious as to be "a breach of faith with the community of mankind" (*ibid.*: 121), Marlow nevertheless emphasizes several times that Jim is "one of us". Jim is not, in this sense, of a kind with the other white crew members, who think nothing of fleeing from the *Patna* or, later, of fleeing from or evading the court of inquiry. Jim, unlike these men, is horrified by his actions. As he says: "It was as if I had jumped into a well – into an everlasting deep hole" (*ibid.*: 87). Moreover, he alone of the crew is prepared to face the inquiry, as he says "to fight this thing down" (*ibid.*: 119). Jim acknowledges his moral responsibility for the ship's passengers and in some sense feels his moral failure deeply; it was not as if he lacked any capacity for moral judgement, even for applying it to himself. Jim is disgusted with the actions of the other crew members and, as it turns out, his own actions. All the same, when the time for action comes he himself has been found wanting, so he finally jumps himself into the crew's lifeboat.

As I say, Jim recognizes his moral failure; indeed, he judges himself in one sense as harshly as, or more harshly than, many of those around him. Yet in another sense we wonder whether he has really seriously reflected on and faced up to his actions at all, and here is the danger of self-deception I alluded to earlier in relation to Murdoch. The way in which Jim responds to his failure of nerve may lead us to certain doubts. So there is the suspicion, for instance, that what troubles Jim most is not what he has done but what he has lost: a supposed right to think of himself in a certain way. As Marlow says, "the idea obtrudes itself that he made so much of his disgrace while it is the guilt alone that matters. He was not – if I may say so – clear to me. He was not clear" (*ibid.*: 135). Then there is the question of why, after the *Patna* affair, Jim should suddenly leave several jobs when his identity becomes clear. Is it that, as Jim says, he will no longer be trusted by his employer, or is he simply running away, running away most fundamentally from himself? Marlow cannot say: "Obviously Jim was not of the winking sort; but what I could never make up my mind about was whether his line of conduct amounted to shirking his ghost or to facing him out" (*ibid.*: 150).

Even in Patusan, where Jim has been sent as a local agent for a trader friend of Marlow, and which seems to be an ideal opportunity for Jim to redeem himself, Marlow's – and our – doubts remain. Things seem to start off well. After ridding the people of the village of a band of outlaws and standing up to the local Raja, Jim is loved and admired by all, his word being law for the people. Jim even wins the heart of a girl, Jewel, the cruelly mistreated stepdaughter of the agent he is there to replace. But questions remain. Consider what Jim says to Marlow when he visits Patusan:

> "The very thought of the world outside is enough to give me a fright; because, don't you see … I have not forgotten why I came here. … Upon my soul and conscience … if such a thing [meaning the *Patna* affair] can be forgotten, then I think that I have a right to dismiss it from my mind … Ask any man here" … his voice changed. "Is it not strange," he went on in a gentle, almost yearning tone, "that all these people, all these people who would do anything for me, can never be made to understand? Never! … What more can I want? If you ask them who is brave – who is true – who is just – who is it they would trust with their lives? – they would say, Tuan Jim. And yet they can never know the real, real truth …". *(Ibid.: 232–3)*

Has Jim really come to terms with or mastered his past weakness, is he really any more self-aware, or does his life in Patusan merely sustain his grand illusions about himself? Even Jim's last acts admit of conflicting interpretations. Here the story takes the form of the letter from Marlow I mentioned earlier, in which Marlow pieces together from conversations with those involved – the outlaw Captain Brown, Jewel and Jim's servant, Tamb' Itam – Jim's last days in Patusan. Jim is away from the village when the outlaw Captain Brown and his crew arrive in Patusan seeking provisions and possible plunder. After an initial exchange of fire with the villagers, Brown establishes a base for himself on a knoll by the river. When Jim returns he goes out to meet Brown. For his part, Brown realizes that he is hopelessly outnumbered against an organized people in the charge of another white man whom they venerate and will follow almost without question. But as it turns out Brown has one advantage. Interpreting events as he learns of them from Brown later when Brown is on his deathbed, Marlow says that "Brown

... had a satanic gift of finding out the best and the weakest spot in his victims" (*ibid.*: 295). With Jim he soon finds his way, as Brown says, "to get in and shake his twopenny soul around and inside out and upside down – by God!" (*ibid.*: 294). So putting his case, Brown:

> asked Jim, with a sort of brusque despairing frankness, whether he himself – straight now – didn't understand that when "it came to saving one's life in the dark, one didn't care who else went – three, thirty, three hundred people" – it was as if a demon had been whispering advice in his ear.   (*Ibid.*: 295–6)

So Jim convinces the villagers to provide Brown and his men with safe passage down river to the coast, and is betrayed by Brown who takes his revenge for a life of "ill-luck" by taking a backwater to the coast so as to surprise and kill the armed villagers charged with monitoring his departure. Among the casualties is Jim's friend Dain Waris, son of the main chieftain Doramin, who had trusted in Jim's advice. Outraged, the villagers turn on Jim and it is clear that he will have to fight them. But Jim will not fight, even as Jewel begs him to. Instead he goes out to meet Doramin, who shoots him dead.

Does Jim, in going out to meet Doramin, display the kind of qualities that failed him when the opportunity arose on the *Patna*? Or is his refusal to fight one last expression of that same failure to act? Marlow cannot say, finding Jim inscrutable to the last. To be sure, Jim goes out to face his own death, but as Marlow sees it, "at the call of his exalted egoism. He goes away from a living woman to celebrate his pitiless wedding with a shadowy ideal of conduct. Is he satisfied – quite, now, I wonder? We ought to know. He is one of us" (*ibid.*: 318). But we do not know; we wonder too, and that is central to the point, as I see it, of an appreciation of Conrad's novel.

## "He is one of us"

I have suggested that we may doubt whether Jim ever really does come to terms with his actions on the *Patna*: whether he learns from this experience. But what makes Jim's case and our doubts about him significant is the suggestion, repeated many times throughout *Lord Jim* and as indicated in the previous quote, that Jim is "one of us". Marlow sees Jim in this way from first sight: "I liked his appearance; I knew his appearance; he came from the right place; he was one of us" (*ibid.*: 35). And later: "He was a youngster of the sort you like to see about you; of the sort you like to imagine yourself to have been" (*ibid.*: 99). But the sense of fellowship goes deeper than that. Describing his last moments on the *Patna*, Jim attempts to account for his actions before Marlow, who is moved as follows:

> I can't explain to you who haven't seen him ... the mixed nature of my feelings. ... He appealed to all sides at once – to the side turned perpetually to the light of day, and to that side of us which, like the other hemisphere of the moon, exists stealthily in perpetual darkness ... He swayed me ... The occasion was obscure, insignificant – what you will: a lost youngster, one in a million – but then he was one of us; an incident as completely devoid of importance as the flooding of an ant-heap, and yet the mystery of his attitude got hold of me as though he had been an individual in the forefront of his kind, as if the obscure truth involved were momentous enough to affect mankind's conception of itself. (*Ibid.*: 73)

What pervades *Lord Jim*, and what makes Jim most significantly "one of us", is itself doubt. Of course we have doubts about Jim's character. But beyond this there is another doubt we might have, one that it is our natural tendency to resist but which the novel moves us to recognize: a doubt about our own character, a doubt about ourselves. Visiting Patusan Marlow attempts to reassure Jewel that Jim will not leave, that "the world did not want him, it had forgotten him, it would not even know him" (*ibid.*: 243). When Jewel repeatedly asks "why", this is Marlow's reply, as related to his dinner companions:

> "Because he is not good enough," I said brutally ... Without raising her voice, she threw into it an infinity of scathing contempt, bitterness, and despair.
> "This is the very thing he said.... You lie!" ...

> "Hear me out!" I entreated … "Nobody, nobody is good enough". (*Ibid.*)

As Marlow says shortly after to his dinner companions, Jim:

> "told me he was satisfied … nearly. This is going further than most of us dare. I – who have the right to think myself good enough – dare not. Neither does any of you here, I suppose? …"
>
> Marlow paused, as if expecting an answer. Nobody spoke.
>
> "Quite right," he began again. "Let no soul know, since the truth can be wrung out of us only by some cruel, little, awful catastrophe. But he is one of us, and he could say he was satisfied … nearly." (*Ibid.*: 248)

To say that Jim is "one of us" is not to suggest that we understand him. On the contrary, we do not really understand Jim at all, and that is my point. In this respect many philosophical – as well as literary – interpretations of *Lord Jim* do not really take a certain ambiguity about Jim in this novel seriously enough, seeking in effect to resolve it in one way or another. I shall focus on two of the more notable philosophical interpretations. Daniel Brudney argues that Jim's behaviour is explained by a kind of narcissistic self-obsession, which makes him dependent on how others see him and suggestible in their presence, so that "[h]e jumps from the *Patna* at the repeated urging of the men already in the lifeboat" and, further, that he "sees his suicide as the right action only or at least primarily due to his continuing narcissistic blinders" (1998: 268–9).[8] Richard Eldridge argues that Jim is initially fatally flawed by "pride, self-love and [moral] exceptionalism" (1989: 90), but is morally transformed on Patusan. So Eldridge suggests Jim's final act in going out to meet Doramin and face the "surviving political and moral authority" expresses his "respect for persons" so that here Jim "may well be acting from [a Kantian] understanding of duty" (*ibid*:. 95–7).[9] Yet, as both Brudney and Eldridge concede, the meaning of Jim's final act remains ambiguous. So, Conrad leaves it open that Jim's final act may be "a last flicker of superb egoism" ([1900] 2007: 315). But now if Jim's final act remains so stubbornly ambiguous, one may question whether trying in a more general way to resolve for ourselves the ambiguity about Jim's character is the right, or at least the most illuminating, way to read this novel.[10] At least to my mind, *Lord Jim* is hardly amenable to such attempts at resolution. Moreover, while we may want, perhaps led on by Marlow's repeated questioning, to understand the kind of man Jim is, to understand his character, what makes him act in the way that he does, there is an invitation in *Lord Jim* to question our motives for this. Consider again Marlow's attitude to Jim and his desire, as he says, to find "a shadow of excuse" for him. Looking for one, he questions the hospitalized and delirious chief engineer who has avoided the inquiry:

> Did I believe in a miracle? and why did I desire it so ardently? Was it for my own sake that I wished to find some shadow of excuse for that young fellow … whose appearance alone added a touch of personal concern to the thoughts suggested by the knowledge of his weakness – made it a thing of mystery and terror – like a hint of a destructive fate ready for us all whose youth – in its day – had resembled his youth? I fear that such was the secret motive of my prying. I was, and no mistake, looking for a miracle. (*Ibid.*: 41)

Marlow's words here suggest that our motives in trying to render Jim's character clear and unambiguous might lead us astray: that they may be concerned less with finding out the truth than with reassuring ourselves, insulating ourselves from the "hint of a destructive fate ready for us all" that Jim represents. Considering Marlow's question to his dinner companions, for example, it may be that we need to think that we *are* good enough, that we would not jump should we face such a "cruel, little, awful catastrophe". But to think that we need to fix Jim's character once and for all in our minds. Only then can we say, for example, that Jim's failure is explained by a kind of narcissism and in so doing convince ourselves that we are (or would be, or can be) prepared where Jim was not. But while we may want to put distance between us (our character) and Jim, the effect of the kind of ambiguity and thus doubt that Conrad leaves surrounding Jim prevents that. Yet much of the commentary on this novel can be seen as an attempt to establish just this kind of distance.

## Learning to think – about ourselves

The point we might draw from *Lord Jim* is an uncomfortable one. I have already noted Diamond's suggestion that the capacity to make certain distinctions we might achieve through our experience of literature, such as the distinction between "what is alive, and what is shallow, sentimental, cheap" amounts to "a kind of learning to think". What I would add to that now is that learning to think depends also on an awareness of the ways in which this process might be distorted by our own particular weaknesses, evasions, moral frailties. In judging and acting we need to be aware of, so as not to discount, "that side of us which … exists stealthily in perpetual darkness". If Jim's character and motives remain dark to us, so, we might come to realize, may our own. I agree with Diamond and others that imaginative literature plays an important part in developing and strengthening our moral sensibility, but beyond this our response to literature, and in particular a novel like *Lord Jim*, can bring home to us the gaps that inevitably exist for us in that moral sensibility. *Lord Jim* reminds us that we can never be entirely sure of ourselves, "since the truth can be wrung out of us only by some cruel, little, awful catastrophe". It is part of what it is to have a developed, we might also say mature, moral sensibility that we do not discount the possibility that faced with such a catastrophe we might fail the test; a real sense of that possibility is itself, I suggest, part of learning to think.

To expand on the above point, what *Lord Jim* may suggest, in line with certain recent arguments in moral philosophy and moral psychology, is that moral character is much less influential than we commonly like to believe.[11] There is well-known empirical evidence that suggests, first, that we have a strong tendency to ascribe stable and consistent personality traits to people and, second, that our predictions about how people will act based on such ascriptions often prove to be mistaken. So whether or not a person acts in accordance with virtue (or simply does the right thing) has been shown to depend heavily – despite intuitions to the contrary – on factors to do with certain features of the situation that person is in. In one famous experiment, whether a person stops to help a distressed colleague was found to depend not on their supposed personality traits but on whether or not they were in a hurry.[12] This is not to say that there is no such thing as character or that character, or at least certain settled dispositions to action, are never explanatory of people's behaviour.[13] Nevertheless, when we turn to consider Jim's situation on the *Patna* we may be struck by how extraordinary and stressful it must have been for him. As Peter Goldie says in a related discussion of *Lord Jim*, "what an extreme test Jim had to face! Who, we might wonder, would have been strong and courageous enough to withstand it?" (2004: 94).

Given my reading of *Lord Jim*, Goldie's question is the right kind of question to ask. But, and as Goldie also seems to suggest, the problem with Jim is not just that he was not as courageous as he thought, but that he fails to recognize how his own motives may remain dark to him. In this way Jim *continues* to discount the possibility of moral failure. So he says to Marlow that in Patusan "if I go straight nothing can touch me ... frankly, don't you think I am pretty safe? It all depends upon me, and ... I have lots of confidence in myself" ([1900] 2007: 248). But what all Jim's confidence rests on is his hope, as he says, for a "clean slate", a hope really for something impossible; Jim's hope is almost that the events on the *Patna* should not have happened, certainly that they should not have marked him, determined him to some extent. But they have marked him and the revengeful but intuitive Captain Brown soon finds the spot; in the end a few carefully chosen words from Brown are enough to undo Jim, to unravel all he has achieved (or seemingly achieved) in Patusan. I suggested above that *Lord Jim* reminds us how we can never be entirely sure of ourselves, so in one sense we are no safer than Jim. Yet to *seriously* believe this – to take this knowledge to heart – can perhaps make a difference to how we fare in life. At the very least, if Jim had had any real sense that he was *not* safe, he might have been more prepared for Captain Brown.

The fact that we cannot be sure that we are safe from some unexpected moral catastrophe does not show that we cannot judge Jim, even condemn his cowardice. But this fact should lead us to consider the attitude we take up towards Jim that is manifest in the manner in which we judge him; here the fact that Jim's failure could be our failure is significant. One way we might register our similar vulnerability is through our pity for Jim, the kind of pity that is registered when one is inclined to say "There but for the grace of God go I". However, it is not so easy to seriously entertain the possibility that we might ourselves behave in a way comparable to Jim on his worst day, with gross cowardice or with something (who can tell?) just as bad.[14] To put the point differently, and remembering my argument in Chapter 3, serious moral reflection, reflection I should like to add now quite apart from that leading to moral judgement, is difficult in the sense that it requires the will to be honestly and rigorously self-critical. What I am suggesting is that it is through our responses to a work like *Lord Jim*, through our conflicting responses to such a work, that we can gain a sense of what serious moral reflection really requires of us: of the kind of unflinching scrutiny it requires, scrutiny not most fundamentally of others but of *ourselves*. A failure to subject ourselves to this kind of scrutiny is itself a kind of evasion of serious moral reflection. Moreover, it is an evasion that may itself be supported by what I am suggesting is a too narrow conception of moral thought, one that focuses merely on moral judgement.

Given the above argument, we can see how moral philosophical readings of *Lord Jim* may obscure our understanding and appreciation of this novel. To explain, consider a kind of argument *against* the idea that it is in the nature of (some) literature – as opposed to philosophy, say – to convey important truths. As Lamarque says:

> To read philosophy is to read for truth. In contrast, to read and value a work *from a literary point of view* seems quite different … literary works that are too overtly didactic, that too obviously are trying to impart a message, are seldom valued highly. (2009: 253–4)

On Lamarque's final point I am inclined to say: just so. But the problem may be with overt didacticism or the *quality* of the thought rather than with the suggestion that literature *as literature* might convince us of important truths. It is the quality of thought that literature demands from both writers *and* readers that has concerned me in this chapter; and, as Diamond notes, as distinct from the attention demanded by philosophical argument, "critical attention to the character and quality of thought in a work may be asked of a reader in many other ways as well". One difference between philosophy and literature is brought out in our differing attitudes towards ambiguity in literature as opposed to philosophy (at least in its analytic variety). Not only is there no demand that Conrad, *as a writer of literature,* resolve the ambiguity surrounding Jim, but moral philosophical readings that do so – that do what Conrad has declined to do – may themselves seem (and make Conrad seem) overly didactic because they are insufficiently attuned to the "character and quality of thought" that literature demands of us as readers. Thus they may fail to capture not only much that is of (aesthetic) interest or value in a given work, but also what we might (morally) learn from it.

*Lord Jim* illustrates a dimension of moral thought that goes beyond making judgements and in so doing reveals how our moral thought and the judgements that may flow from that may end up being merely moralistic, in the sense that in condemning or excusing Jim we may fail the real challenge of moral thought that *Lord Jim* invites, which is to reflect on the possibility that we might fail as Jim did. Conrad himself, I think, was keenly aware of the demands of moral thought and reflection in this sense. Consider, for example, the following passage from a letter from Conrad to one of his readers about his novel *Victory,* a passage that deals explicitly with the issue of ambiguity in literature:

> [A] work of art is very seldom limited to one exclusive mean-
> ing and not necessarily tending to a definite conclusion ... as
> to precision of images and analysis my artistic conscience is at
> rest. I have given there all the truth that is in me ... But as to
> "final effect" my conscience has nothing to do with that. It is
> the critic's affair to bring to its contemplation his own honesty,
> his sensibility and intelligence. The matter for his conscience
> is just his judgement.
>
> (Letter to B. H. Clark, in Ingram 1986: 89)

The matter for the reader's conscience is indeed his judgement, but his judgement in the wider sense that concerns me here, which importantly involves reflecting on our own response to Jim and specifically our possible desire either to condemn or excuse him.

To expand on the above point, far from being a flaw, the ambiguity surrounding Jim is a mark of the quality of Conrad's thought. Suresh Raval suggests in his reading of *Lord Jim* that "for Marlow the success of his narrative is closely interwoven with his admission of its failure to clearly grasp Jim", and that "[r]eal failure would consist in the possibility that, given the inscrutable nature of Jim's experience, no attempt is made to record and articulate it for us" (1981: 388–9). Jim's inscrutability is important in my reading of *Lord Jim* since it encourages us to reflect on the possibility that Jim represents for us – as Raval also says, "Marlow sees that if the unexpected erupted in Jim's life, it could occur in anyone else's life" (*ibid.*) – that is, to reflect on the ways in which our own character and motives may remain dark to us. To that extent the core of *Lord Jim* is Marlow and his response to Jim; when Marlow says, "the mystery of his attitude got hold of me as though he had been an individual in the forefront of his kind, as if the obscure truth involved were momentous enough to affect mankind's conception of itself", what he means, I think, is that Jim's story is enough to effect *his* conception of himself. That is why, I suggest, Jim's story "got hold" of Marlow, as it may get hold of us.

I do not want to suggest though that *Lord Jim* necessarily will, or even ought to, get hold of anyone who reads it in the manner I have suggested. Whether it does will depend on the kind of self-conception we are prompted to reflect on. So far I have focused on Marlow's experiences of, and reflections on, Jim: on his perspective on Jim. But another perspective on Jim is provided by a certain French lieutenant that Marlow happens to meet years after the *Patna* affair. This lieutenant, we learn, was on board the ship, the *Avondale*, that finally rescued the *Patna* and, further, that he spent thirty hours on board the *Patna* with two quartermasters while it was towed safely to port. Faced with the same crisis this man simply does what needs to be done: as he says, "one's possible" ([1900] 2007: 109). As he also says, "Brave – you conceive – in the Service – one has got to be – the trade demands it" (*ibid.*: 113). For this lieutenant, saving the *Patna* was simply what the situation and the trade called for; he cannot at first even remember the name of the *Patna*. The lieutenant has not heard of Jim's actions on the *Patna* and, as Marlow recounts them, the lieutenant appears sympathetic, as he says to Marlow, "The fear, the fear – look you – it is always there" (*ibid.*: 112). But when Marlow says that he is glad to see the lieutenant "taking a lenient view" (*ibid.*: 114), he is left disappointed by the lieutenant's reply:

> I contended that one may get on knowing very well that
> one's courage does not come of itself ... But the honour – the
> honour, *monsieur!* ... The honour ... that is real – that is! And
> what life may be worth when ... when the honour is gone ... I
> can offer no opinion. I can offer no opinion – because – *mon-
> sieur* – I know nothing of it.               (*Ibid.*: 114)

The French lieutenant's view of the matter is both simpler and
harsher: what matters is the honour and Jim has lost his. The lieutenant
is not concerned to look into Jim's soul, to discover the "obscure truth"
about him in the specific sense that troubles Marlow. Marlow reflects
that where Jim is concerned it is "as if the obscure truth involved were
momentous enough to affect mankind's conception of itself", but there
appears to be no such threat to the lieutenant's conception of mankind
or himself; he is happy, for instance, to claim: "Man is born a coward"
(*ibid.*: 113). Yet this, we must remember, is from a man who spent thirty
hours on a ship that could sink at any moment! The French lieutenant,
one might say, is a man who harbours no illusions about the fragil-
ity of character and what that might mean for a particular life. The
exchange between Marlow and the French lieutenant suggests another
response to the events that Conrad has portrayed. Moreover, it seems
from the text – from Marlow's admiration for the lieutenant and for his
interest in the lieutenant's opinion of the affair with Jim – that Conrad
himself has respect for this practical man of action; he was, as Marlow
says, "one of those steady, reliable men who are the raw material of
great reputations, one of those uncounted lives that are buried without
drums and trumpets under the foundations of monumental successes"
(*ibid.*: 110–11). What the example of the French lieutenant shows, I
think, is that the kind of self-understanding we might gain from *Lord
Jim* depends on our own character as manifest in the way in which we
respond to it: Jim's story may get hold of us as it does Marlow, but as
with the French lieutenant it may not get hold of us in quite this way.[15]
That Jim's story does get hold of us, or how it does, says something
about us. The French lieutenant is happy to accept that courage does
not come of itself, but that, including all that it entails, is not something
everyone will be happy to accept; as with Marlow, the very fact of Jim
may affect our conception of ourselves.

Still, one may take Marlow's ultimate dissatisfaction with the French lieutenant's account of Jim as a mark of the lieutenant's failure of moral reflection. On this point my interpretation of the French lieutenant contrasts sharply with that offered by Eldridge in the work I have referred to. In contrast to what I have suggested, Eldridge argues that the lieutenant's character too is marked by "a narcissistic exceptionalism", as well as "pride and [a] sense of special moral purity" (1989: 81). I find this reading implausible, for the lieutenant more or less states that he is in no way exceptional; as he says, "there is a point – for the best of us – there is somewhere a point when you let go everything … Given a certain combination of circumstances, fear is sure to come" ([1900] 2007: 113). These are hardly the words of a man who claims special moral purity.[16] Eldridge notes the lieutenant's admission that "he shares fear with everyone", but thinks nevertheless that the lieutenant "claims unlike the many to 'know nothing' of dishonourable action" (1989: 81). But while the lieutenant says that he does not know what life is worth "when the honour is gone", he does not claim to know nothing of dishonourable *action*, and in fact the lieutenant actually alludes to a certain dishonourable act of his own: "even a simple headache or a fit of indigestion … is enough to … Take me, for instance – I have made my proofs. *Eh bien!* I, who am speaking to you, once" ([1900] 2007: 113). But draining his glass he moves on without elucidating further.

## Conclusion

One might be tempted to say that Jim's life was shattered by nothing more than a momentary weakness, a failure (but was it momentary?) of the kind of immediate moral responsiveness to others that I discussed earlier. But of course Jim's failure depended – as my question in parenthesis suggests – on more than that. It was Jim's inability to fully acknowledge the moral significance of such immediate primitive responsiveness in life generally, and that this cannot be counted on, that brings him down. If we look at Jim's life after his moment of weakness simply from the point of view of the moral judgements he makes (including about himself) and the principles he believes in and serves (including giving his life up to the service of the people of Patusan) then it is hard to find moral fault with him.[17] But in order to see Jim accurately, to see the particular failure of moral thought or reflection to which he has fallen victim, we need to look beyond this to all that Jim says and does. We need to look, to give just a few examples, to his leaving several jobs once his identity becomes clear, to his peculiar insistence that in Patusan he is "safe" and to his decision to let Captain Brown leave Patusan.

To explain further, what Jim needs (but lacks) is not any wider grasp of moral concepts or theories or the ability to make moral judgements on that basis, but – and among other things – the capacity to ask certain questions of himself: questions of a kind to which he (like any of us) may have no entirely satisfactory answer, such as "Why am I running?", "Am I safe?" and "Why does Brown's plight move me?"; questions, moreover, that involve (remembering the discussion of Chapter 3) Jim in *reflecting on the meaning of his own actions or responses*. These are of course Jim's questions, but Jim is, we may come to see, "one of us", so it may be that his questions resonate with, or speak to, us. As Marlow says, "the mystery of his attitude got hold of me". I do not say that Jim's story should "get hold of" you, but only that it may do; here is one way literature can help us learn to think. My point is that such thinking does have a practical import.

Still, one might wonder what the practical import of such reflection might be. I have said that in so far as *Lord Jim* gets hold of us it shows us that we are not entirely safe, as Marlow says, from such a "cruel, little, awful catastrophe". But what, one might ask, is the practical value of knowing that? Indeed, a serious sense of it may be thought to be, contrary to what I have suggested, quite paralysing; far from enabling effective responses to morally challenging situations, such reflection might be thought to stand in the way of such responses. I have suggested that *Lord Jim* may show us that we can never be entirely sure about ourselves, but of course that is not a doubt one should entertain when it is imperative to act. However, it is a doubt we might – and perhaps should – entertain in reflecting on our responses after the crisis has passed. *Lord Jim* begins with Jim's first experience of a crisis at sea, the kind of crisis he has been waiting for in order to show his quality. The young Jim is on a training ship for officers of the mercantile marine when there is a collision between a coaster and an anchored schooner in the middle of a gale. While Jim stands still on the deck several of the other trainee boys rush past him to man the cutter and set out in rescue. Jim does not end up in the cutter. "Too late, youngster", the captain tells him, gripping his shoulder. "Better luck next time. This will teach you to be smart" ([1900] 2007: 9). An opportunity lost, it would seem; Jim was not quick enough. What Jim does not think to ask is: "Was it just that I was not quick enough?" This, in the end, is how Jim views the situation after the fact when the bowman of the cutter is celebrated below deck as a hero for saving a man in the water:

> Jim thought it a pitiful display of vanity. The gale had minis-
> tered to a heroism as spurious at its own pretence of terror. He
> felt angry with the brutal tumult of earth and sky for taking
> him unawares and checking unfairly a generous readiness
> for narrow escapes. Otherwise he was rather glad he had not
> gone into the cutter, since a lower achievement had served the
> turn. He had enlarged his knowledge more than those who
> had done the work. When all men flinched, then – he felt sure
> – he alone would know how to deal with the spurious menace
> of wind and seas. He knew what to think of it.    (*Ibid.*: 9–10)

But has Jim "enlarged his knowledge"?! Yes, we can never be entirely sure of ourselves, but Jim's lack of critical self-reflection, his inability to attend to the possible meaning of his own responses as indicated above, makes him totally unprepared for the challenges he thinks he will so easily meet. It may be that there is some unholy combination of our own particular character and circumstance that would undo any one of us; the French lieutenant of Conrad's story certainly thought so. But that is not to say that the kind of critical self-reflection I am highlighting counts for nothing in practical terms. Not all failures are so life altering as Jim's on the *Patna*; as a trainee Jim just does not end up in the cutter. In such cases – and they are many and varied – it is all too easy to think that we were taken "unawares" and "unfairly" so, whereas what we may need to reflect on – and here again I am talking as I did in Chapter 3 of reflecting on our own responses – is the possibility that we are not, and that might just mean *not yet*, up to the challenge, whatever that might be.

# SIX

# Moral difference

At the end of the previous chapter I suggested that moral reflection involves more than a grasp of moral concepts or theories and the ability to make moral judgements on that basis: specifically, that it involved the capacity to ask certain questions of oneself. My focus there was on the many ways in which our own character (and weakness) may remain dark to us and how serious moral reflection requires a certain capacity for self-scrutiny. But an aspect of such questioning that I did not so much highlight there is the essentially personal nature of such reflections on at least some occasions. What a person is attempting to find out about in such reflection on such occasions, I shall argue, is something about themselves, about their particular character.[1] But the point here is not, or so I shall now argue, restricted to finding out the ways in which we might fall short of the character we imagine ourselves to possess. Beyond this, such reflection may involve finding out the *kind* of moral character we possess. To talk in terms of kinds of character is to suggest that in a given situation agents with different moral characters might appropriately reach different moral judgements about how to act. In this chapter I shall advance the case for thinking that moral reflection and judgement might, at least sometimes, be personal in this more radical sense.[2] There is no suggestion in this kind of situation that in judging others a person does not hold themselves to the same standards or that they lack the kind of capacity for self-scrutiny in quite the way I suggested in the previous chapter; I am not suggesting they are moralistic in these kinds of ways. Rather, my suggestion will be that in supposing that anyone in the same situation should reach the same moral judgement we fail to attend to what is involved on at least some occasions in reaching a moral judgement *in our own case* about how we ought to act. Thus, I hope to highlight once again how certain conceptions of moral thought, including those shared by the kind of impartialist theories I considered in Chapter 4, may be inadequate so that our moral judgements (of others) fall short of the standards required for serious moral thought and reflection and are, to that extent, moralistic.

## Moral judgement and universalizability

What I am suggesting is that moral judgements are not always universalizable. The idea that moral judgements are universalizable lies at the heart of the impartialist moral theories that I considered in Chapter 4. Somewhat more broadly it may seem to be essential to the idea that moral theory – of whatever stripe – exhaustively determines moral judgement. My argument against universalizability is bound to strike some as highly contentious. It does, however, have the merit at least of making clear my objections to a very common conception of the nature of moral judgement, a conception that misrepresents quite fundamentally the nature of moral reflection and judgement as I shall understand it. The idea that moral judgements are not always universalizable is hardly new. It is an idea that was defended by Winch forty years ago in his influential although much-contested article "The Universalizability of Moral Judgments" (1972). Moreover, the account of moral deliberation and judgement that Winch defends there is in ways strikingly similar to an account offered by Williams much later (see esp. Williams 1993) and which helps to further explain Williams's objection to what he has called the morality system, which I discussed in Chapter 4.

So to begin, what exactly is the claim that moral judgements are not universalizable? As Winch puts the point:

> [I]f A says "X is the right thing for me to do" and if B, in a situation not relevantly different, says "X is the wrong thing

for me to do", it can be that both are correct. That is, it may be that neither what each says, nor anything entailed by what each says, contradicts anything said or implied by the other.

(1972: 164–5)

Winch is not saying that two conflicting moral judgements are both correct *simpliciter*. Winch's point is that in the kind of situation he envisages we need to ask: correct for whom? Central to Winch's argument is the way in which he thinks a person's character will appropriately determine their moral judgement. Winch illustrates what is at issue by drawing on an example from Herman Melville's novella *Billy Budd*. What interests Winch in this story is the moral conflict faced by Captain Vere of the HMS *Indomitable* in the case of the court martial and execution of Billy Budd. Winch wants to say that the conflict Vere faces, in reaching the decision to sentence Billy to death, is "a conflict between two genuinely moral 'oughts', a conflict, that is, *within* morality" (*ibid.*: 158–9). On the one hand, Vere, in his speech at Billy's court martial, accepts that Billy is "innocent before God"; Billy's action in striking and accidentally killing his superior, Claggart, was caused by frustration born of the intolerable persecution he suffered at the hands of that man. But, on the other hand, the enforcement of military law relating to such an action, on the high seas and maybe especially at a time (such as this was) when the threat of mutiny was acute, was also for Vere a moral obligation.

Now Winch holds *both* that morally he (Winch) could not in such circumstances have condemned a man "innocent before God" *and* that, in deciding to condemn Billy, "Vere did what was, for him, the right thing to do" (*ibid.*: 163–4). Winch argues that "[i]n reaching this decision [that he could not condemn Billy] I do not think that I should appeal to any considerations over and above those to which Vere himself appeals" (*ibid.*: 163). Winch argues, that is, that there is no failure on either Vere's or his part to recognize some consideration relevant to judgement that might then explain their divergence here. According to Winch, what it is right for Vere to do in this situation is not necessarily what is right for him (i.e. Winch) to do in this situation; in this kind of case moral judgements are not universalizable. As Winch says, there is "a certain class of *first-person* moral judgments ... not subject to the universalizability principle" (*ibid.*: 159).

## First-person moral judgements

To explain why Winch should think that there is a class of first-person moral judgements that are not subject to the universalizability principle we need to consider his account of the nature of moral deliberation in the kind of case he envisages. Those cases are of course where we are thinking about the moral judgements of others. As Winch says:

> [W]hen I think about the moral decisions and dilemmas of others, it seems to me that I am very often asking: "What would *I* think it right to do in such a situation?" That is, I am making a hypothetical agent's judgment of my own. Thus, only a man who is himself a moral agent, who is capable of making moral decisions of his own, is capable of making and understanding spectators' moral judgments about the actions of other people. (*Ibid.*: 153–4)

The reason, Winch wants to stress, that we need to be able to make our own moral decisions in order to be able to make any spectator judgement about the actions of others is that the manner in which we reach judgements *as agents* will determine the nature and scope of our spectator moral judgements. But in order to see how this is we need to consider in some detail the kinds of factor on which an agent's own moral decisions may turn. So recall now Winch's own judgement concerning Billy Budd.

Remember first of all that in the case of Billy Budd's court martial Winch is reflecting on what it would be right for him to do, given that he is faced with two conflicting moral oughts. That Winch should ask "What ought I to do?" here does show that he thinks that there is a morally correct decision for him to make in this case. There is, Winch wants to say, something that an agent has to find out. But Winch's point is that his decision is correct only for him and not necessarily correct for another in his place; while Winch gives precedence to one moral consideration (Billy's innocence) over another (military law), he is not saying that anyone else in the same place must weigh these considerations as he does. For this reason, reaching a moral decision in a case like this does not amount to simply dissolving the conflict. The importance of Winch's asking "What would *I* think it right to do in such a situation?" is just that, through imagining himself acting in this situation – having to convict or, otherwise, acquit Billy Budd – he may discover what is, as we shall see, *morally possible* for him in this situation. As Winch says:

> I try ... to confine myself to the genuinely moral features of the situation. Having done this, I believe that I could not have acted as did Vere; and by the "could not", I do not mean "should not have had the nerve to", but that I should have found it morally impossible to condemn a man "innocent before God" under such circumstances. (*Ibid.*: 163)

In a case like this, an agent's *decision* that he morally cannot act in some way is thus, puzzling as this may sound, a *discovery* about what it is right for that agent to do. As Winch says, "deciding what to do is, in a situation like this, itself a sort of finding out what is the right thing to do" (*ibid.*: 165). For an agent's decision here concerns what is *morally possible for them in particular*. As Winch later says, "what one finds out [in a case like this] is something about oneself, rather than anything one can speak of as holding universally" (*ibid.*: 168). The crux of Winch's argument is, then, that a person's moral judgement in such cases may turn on what is personally morally possible for them. In order to assess Winch's argument, therefore, it is necessary to consider his account of such moral modalities, and it is to this account that I now turn.

## Moral incapacity

To begin, one might argue that if the above is a true account of Winch's judgement then that judgement has no moral worth. For surely the decision here turns not on any moral consideration but merely on Winch's psychological capacities and incapacities. But what is crucial for Winch is that when he says he could not convict a man innocent before God he is not referring to a mere psychological incapacity (it is not, as he says, that he "lacks the nerve" to convict) but what we might call a genuine *moral* incapacity, an incapacity that is itself expressive (in a way that mere psychological incapacities are not) of Winch's particular moral character. We may illustrate the difference between moral and mere psychological incapacities as follows. If, to take the case of an obvious psychological incapacity, I were to say that I cannot ride in lifts (e.g. because I am claustrophobic), then it at least makes sense for another to encourage me to try to do this. In the case of genuine moral incapacities, however, to encourage an agent to try to do what he says he cannot do is, as Winch says elsewhere in this connection, not to meet the agent's point "so much as making a black, tasteless joke" (1987: 158). To suggest that Winch should try to overcome his incapacity to convict Billy, for example, is to fail to appreciate that this incapacity is expressive of his particular moral identity or character.

To expand on the point above, imagine that someone were to say to Winch that he should seek the help of a counsellor or perhaps take a swig of brandy and that then perhaps he might find that he was able to do what he says he cannot do. Such a reply would miss Winch's point since it is not directed at Winch's *reasons* for claiming that he cannot convict Billy: that is, that he cannot convict him because he is a man innocent before God. Having said this, I am not suggesting that someone might *necessarily* be mistaken in asking Winch to consider again the case at hand and the value of the conflicting demands that are involved. For of course it is possible that someone will suspect that Winch has not reflected on the case carefully enough. All I am suggesting is that eventually such reflections (and doubts) will (and should) come to an end: that we may reach a point where it is clear that Winch has considered all the relevant factors and where it no longer makes sense to say that Winch has *failed* adequately to consider, say, some relevant moral demand or value in this case even though it is possible that different agents will weigh those values differently. To continue to press Winch at such a point is simply to reject the idea that there are moral incapacities of the kind Winch is highlighting.

Of course those who oppose Winch's notion of *moral* incapacity can accept that Winch's incapacity is expressive of his character in some sense yet deny that this incapacity is a moral incapacity in the sense outlined above. So one might argue that Winch's incapacity here is expressive merely of a certain weakness or infirmity of character: that his judgement really does indicate a failure of nerve. But this is, as I say, to ignore the relevance of *what it is* Winch says he cannot do here to our understanding of his judgement. What Winch says he cannot do in this kind of circumstance is *convict a man innocent before God*. It is not that he is simply incapable of performing an objectionable duty; rather, his incapacity here is precisely an incapacity to do something that is morally objectionable – to convict a man innocent before God. This helps to explain why it amounts to a kind of "black, tasteless joke" to suggest that Winch should try to do what he says he cannot do. To suggest in a situation like this that a person should try to do what they claim they morally cannot do is to fail to appreciate the significance of certain moral ideas (e.g. concerning natural justice) in founding their particular moral character, that we understand what it is to have a moral identity at all in terms of such incapacities and the moral ideas that are involved in articulating them.[3] And Winch's objection to the universalizability principle is then that our moral identities, our distinctive moral characters, may reasonably differ: that moral ideas such as natural justice or the importance of military justice need not have the same moral weight for different agents in the same situation, so that the moral possibilities may be different for different agents. For Winch, to encourage an agent in a situation like this to do what they claim they cannot do is to try to get them to betray their own distinctive moral character.

Winch's account of moral incapacities as outlined above is, as I noted earlier, strikingly similar to Williams's account and it helps to explain why Williams should object in the ways that he does to the impartialist moral theories. As Williams also says, such incapacities are "incapacities that are themselves an expression of the moral life: the kind of incapacity that is in question when we say of someone, usually in commendation of him, that he could not act or was not capable of acting in certain ways" (1993: 59).[4] Williams likewise sees such incapacities as "expressive of, or grounded in, the agent's character or personal dispositions" (*ibid.*: 60). The way in which both Winch and Williams describe our practical deliberation in the face of conflicting moral demands throws further light on the kind of deliberation an agent may be involved in when they are thinking, for instance, about what they ought to do to help the world's desperately poor, to recall the discussion in Chapter 4. For while it is perfectly understandable in the face of such misery for someone to conclude that they morally *cannot* live in the manner that others in the West do, or that they *must* devote considerable resources to alleviating such poverty, one need not extend the same judgement to just anyone.[5] There are other ways in which a person may conclude that they must commit their lives – to family or to their vocation, for example – that rule out such a sacrifice.

One might argue that such other commitments are not moral commitments narrowly construed so that this is not, as was the case with Winch, a conflict within morality as such. Here two points need to be understood. First, neither Winch nor Williams shares the kind of impartialist universalizing conception of morality that would seek to contrast what we owe to others, which is to say to just anyone (a moral demand), with what at least some of our personal projects and personal relationships *demand of us in particular*. For Winch and Williams, such personal commitments or relationships can feature in our expression of personal *moral* modalities, modalities that give substance to the idea of character. Second, while Winch's example concerns a conflict within morality, his more general point is about the role of character in determining an agent's decision about how to act in situations where that decision is not determined by the relevant impartial reasons for action. So, as Joseph Raz has suggested in his discussion of Winch's argument:

> It is … primarily where matters are underdetermined by reason that we reveal and mould our distinctive individuality, our tastes, our imagination, our sociability, and many of our other, including our moral, characteristics. Winch's claims concern the role of our moral character … Notoriously the morality of right and wrong is not exhaustive. Many moral acts are supererogatory. In these cases the demands of morality are incommensurate with some nonmoral reasons. When this is so regarding, say, charitable giving, or volunteering to help with various good causes, we are not rationally required to choose the moral option, but if we do we prove ourselves generous with our time or money. (Raz 2003: 74)

Again, this is not to say that a person might assign little or no weight whatsoever to the demands placed upon us all by the world's desperately poor, but that it is consistent with acknowledging the demand of the desperately poor for our aid that we do not all assign this demand the same weight that some people do. The point is just that the moral possibilities may be different for different agents: that it does not follow from the fact that $X$ concludes that they morally cannot continue to live in the way that so many of us live in the West that any agent similarly placed must make the same judgement, or conclude that $X$ is mistaken, or conclude that $X$'s judgement is not really a moral judgement at all. It *is* a moral judgement, a moral judgement of a kind that we may call supererogatory, and it is surely a point in favour of Winch's account that it enables us to make good sense of such judgements.

But Winch's point is not simply about supererogatory judgements and Raz's suggestion may be misleading. To say that "matters are underdetermined by reason" might seem to suggest that the kind of supererogatory act described above is merely non-obligatory and in that sense somehow *optional*. But that is not how it will strike the agent; it would misrepresent the judgement of someone who takes it that *no other course of action is open to him* but to spend his life helping the world's poorest to say that his action goes beyond what he sees himself as required to do. In making a third-person judgement we can say, thinking of Winch's point, that the reasons for action do not determine the (supposedly one) correct judgement, but an agent's first-person judgement is that the matter is determined; when Winch says that he could not convict a man innocent before God he is saying, in effect, that there is *no option* for him (that this is not a matter of exercising an option).

The picture of practical deliberation that is represented above assigns within a certain domain – a class of first-person judgements – a primary importance to individual character as it is expressed in the decisions of such individuals. Of course any moral theory will allow some scope for people to live different kinds of life, lives in which people develop their own characters in somewhat distinctive kinds of ways. But the position just outlined is more radical than this; the modalities described above – what an agent says they must or cannot do – are themselves expressive of moral character. And in so far as the modalities expressed are personal, in so far as they express in a given situation what I conclude *I* must or cannot do, it follows that in fact there will be alternative conceptions of the moral life, conceptions that involve responding to competing moral (and other) demands differently depending on the character of, or as we might say the kind of life lived by, the agent in question. This, as I say, offends against a principle fundamental to much moral theorizing: the universalizability principle. Nevertheless, I want to argue now that the conception of practical deliberation and judgement that I have outlined does justice to the basic phenomena, to our understanding of what human life is like, in ways that those approaches that take the universalizability principle for granted fail to.

## The limits of universalizability

I am interested in the limits of the universalizability principle in accounting for moral reflection and judgement, but let me acknowledge from the start the deep hold morality understood as a system of universalizable judgements has on our ways of making sense of the world and of other people. So, for example, the expression by people of the kind of modalities I am concerned with – that they must or cannot act in some way – can confound us. A particularly striking example of this is given in J. M. Coetzee's novel *Disgrace* (2000). After losing his teaching job at the Technical University of Cape Town over an affair with a student, Melanie Isaacs, English literature lecturer David Lurie retreats to his daughter Lucy's farm in the Eastern Cape. Shortly after his arrival, the farm is attacked by three unknown black men, who rob them and gang rape and impregnate Lucy. Lucy reports the theft of their car and possessions but will not report the rape and, later, refuses to call the police when one of the rapists, the youngest, turns up at her black neighbour Petrus's party. It is clear that Petrus knows the boy – it turns out they are related by marriage – and, after leaving the party with Lucy, David has the telephone in his hand to call the police. But Lucy stops him:

> "David, no, don't do it. It's not Petrus's fault. If you call in the police, the evening will be destroyed for him. Be sensible."
>
> He is astonished, astonished enough to turn on his daughter. "For God's sake, why isn't it Petrus's fault? One way or another, it was he who brought in those men in the first place … Really, Lucy, from beginning to end I fail to understand.

I fail to understand why you did not lay *real* charges against them, and now I fail to understand why you are protecting Petrus. Petrus is not an innocent party, Petrus is *with* them."

"Don't shout at me, David. This is my life. I am the one who has to live here. What happened to me is my business, mine alone, not yours, and if there is one right I have it is the right not to be put on trial like this, not to have to justify myself – not to you, not to anyone else."  (*Ibid.*: 133)

While in one sense we might agree that what happened to Lucy was her business alone, in another sense we may agree with David. We may share David's view that Lucy is making a terrible mistake and that these men ought to be brought to justice.

"Lucy, Lucy, I plead with you! You want to make up for the wrongs of the past, but this is not the way to do it. If you fail to stand up for yourself at this moment, you will never be able to hold your head up again ... if you are too delicate to call [the police] in now, then we should never have involved them in the first place. We should just have kept quiet and waited for the next attack. Or cut our own throats."

"Stop it, David! I don't need to defend myself before you. *You don't know what happened.*"

"I don't know?"

"No, you don't begin to know. Pause and think about that."

...

"... I repeat: if you buckle at this point, if you fail, you will not be able to live with yourself. You have a duty to yourself, to the future, to your own self-respect. Let me call the police. Or call them yourself."  (*Ibid.*: 133–4)

As readers it is easy to share David's astonishment; how can Lucy not see, we might think, that she ought to call the police? Or even, how can Lucy not see that she really does have a *duty to herself* to call the police? What is clear is that Lucy understands her situation. She later confesses to fearing that these men will return: "I think I am in their territory. They have marked me. They will come back for me" (*ibid.*:

158). What is also clear is that while she knows she is not safe, her not calling the police, not pressing charges of rape against Petrus's relative, is motivated by her determination to stay, for if she does stay she will need Petrus's protection. When David offers to pay for her to go away to visit her mother in Holland, Lucy refuses saying, "If I leave now, David, I won't come back" (*ibid.*: 157). And when David continues in a letter imploring her to listen to him when he says that she is making a dangerous error, Lucy pushes a note under his door:

> "Dear David, You have not been listening to me … I am a dead person and I do not know yet what will bring me back to life. All I know is that I cannot go away."
>
> "You do not see this, and I do not know what more I can do to make you see." …
>
> "Yes, the road I am following may be the wrong one. But if I leave the farm now I will leave defeated, and I will taste that defeat for the rest of my life." (*Ibid.*: 161)

Lucy is the victim of a terrible crime and the injustice of it, not to mention the abject state in which she is now condemned to live – in fear of the men returning and beholden to Petrus for protection – can so easily lead to the judgement that Lucy is mistaken, even that she does have a duty to herself to make matters (morally) right. Yet while we may be tempted to think that Lucy morally ought to report the rape even if that means she will have to leave, Lucy herself judges that she cannot report the rape *because she cannot leave*, and in this expresses what is possible, including what is morally possible, for her. It is a judgement, once again, that is not universalizable.

One might question whether Lucy's decision to stay expresses the kind of moral modality I am concerned with. So one might argue that Lucy's decision that she cannot leave expresses not a moral but a mere psychological incapacity, as I have characterized it above. In that case, and assuming that we think she ought to call the police, it would make sense to advise Lucy to try to live with the defeat that she implies she cannot live with. Or, if it became clear that Lucy could not in this (psychological) sense live with that, say, that it would sap her will to go on, then we might accept her decision but view this incapacity merely as a constraint on Lucy's deliberation about what she ought to do and not itself the expression of a genuine moral incapacity. Once again, however, I think this reply involves a failure to recognize what it is Lucy says she cannot do: a failure to take seriously the moral dimension of her decision. While the decision to call the police and seek justice, even if that means she will have to leave, is clearly a moral judgement, so too is the decision to find a way, abject though it may be, to stay. For staying is for Lucy, as David acknowledges, itself a point of honour, and not just, we suspect, merely to fight for the life she has made on the farm, but to fight back in the only way she can against what was done to her.

There are many ways to interpret, and much more that might be said about, the events I have related from *Disgrace*,[6] including interpretations that are consistent with the universalizability principle. Of course such an example, open as it is to different interpretations, cannot prove the universalizability principle false. But that is not my point in considering it any more than it was part of Winch's point in considering his example from *Billy Budd*. In this respect, many of Winch's critics have generally misunderstood his point in introducing this example. What Winch's critics have assumed is that *Billy Budd* is supposed to provide directly a kind of counter-example to the universalizability thesis: that this story shows clearly and unambiguously that two agents in a given situation might reach differing moral judgements and both be correct. In response to this it has then been argued that Melville's story does not show this at all. So, Winch's critics argue variously: that Vere made the wrong decision;[7] that Vere made the right decision, meaning the decision that anyone in his situation should reach (see e.g. Kolenda 1975; Alweiss 2003); that we just do not know what it is like to be in Vere's situation and so cannot judge his action either way (see Atwell 1967). But Winch does not intend this example to show *directly* that the universalizability thesis is false. For Winch, it is not what the example itself shows but what his response to the story shows that is important here. That is, Winch is drawing our attention to the way in which he reaches a judgement about Vere's decision, and what Winch says about that is relevant to my example as well.

What I want to draw attention to with the example from *Disgrace* is what is required of us if we are to reach a judgement about Lucy's decision. And the best way to explain that is to consider David, who clearly does not understand what is required of him. To begin with, David says continually that he cannot understand his daughter's decision, but his incomprehension is in part due to his inability to think of this decision as *her* decision. As Lucy says to David: "You keep misreading me. Guilt and salvation are abstractions. I don't act in terms of abstractions. Until you make an effort to see that, I can't help you" (2000: 112). Indeed, David's appeal to Lucy is an appeal to supposed abstract, impartial duties that Lucy has – to herself, the future and her self-respect; he appears blind to the first-personal nature of her decision. The point is, as Winch suggests, that in cases like this the judgements we might make as spectators (of the first-person moral judgements of others) depend on our capacity to make comparable first-person moral judgements ourselves, and to see the point we need to recollect the kind of (personal) moral modalities that Winch thinks will be involved in those first-person moral judgements. What that requirement shows in this case is the gap that David would have to bridge to attempt to understand his daughter's decision and make a judgement about it. The point is not that a man cannot be a victim of rape; it is rather that David either cannot or will not put himself in Lucy's place.

It must be acknowledged that there *are* obstacles to putting oneself in another's place in such a case – it is hard to imagine the horror of the events Coetzee portrays – and that may lead to scepticism about whether we are able to make judgements about the moral decisions of others in such extreme cases. But it is possible to resist such scepticism. Moreover, it is important that we do so, since such scepticism is a general threat to our attempts to make moral sense of the lives of others, including by making judgements about their particular moral decisions. Winch's point is that if we *are* to make judgements about the moral decisions of others, then even in such cases one has to be able to make a first-person judgement about oneself in the same situation, since it is only through imagining oneself in another's place that one grasps what the decision might turn on: that it might turn on something about us, our particular character. But, as I say, in David's case it is not simply that it is difficult for him, as it would be for almost anyone, to imagine being in Lucy's place; beyond this David is unwilling, or perhaps unable, to even attempt this imaginative exercise. Apposite here, and perhaps part of the explanation for David's failure, is that putting himself in Lucy's place would be uncomfortably close to putting himself in Melanie's place as well. This is not to say that the situations are identical; he did not rape Melanie but, as David admits, thinking of their second sexual encounter, the affair was not entirely consensual either, "[n]ot rape, not quite that, but undesired nevertheless, undesired to the core" (*ibid.*: 25). So David's abstractions can be seen as a kind of avoidance, as a failure to put himself in a position from which he could make a judgement about Lucy's decision and possibly accept that it was the right one for her to make.

Of course the defender of the universalizability thesis may argue that all the example shows is that David fails to understand Lucy's *situation*. Against this I can only stress again the personal nature of Lucy's decision; she complains not that David does not understand her situation, but that he does not understand *her*. Lucy says in response to David, "if I leave the farm now I will leave defeated, and I will taste that defeat for the rest of my life." Lucy is inviting David to consider not her situation, but *having to act* as he is proposing and in particular what that would amount to for her. To explain the point further, what Winch is suggesting in "The Universalizability of Moral Judgements" is that if I am to make a judgement about Vere's decision to convict Billy Budd, I have to imagine *myself* having to act. But, and here is Winch's point, I can imagine acting only *as the person I am*. So it is not that I now see the situation from Vere's point of view, but that I see *myself* in that hard place and I must decide to do one of two things: convict or acquit. So it is in the case of *Disgrace*; before I can judge Lucy I need to imagine myself faced with her decision. Yet when I do think in this way, the way in which I reach my decision shows that universalizability is not the kind of formal or necessary feature of moral judgement that defenders of the universalizability thesis suppose. In Lucy's place I would find it morally impossible to stay on the terms available to her but that indicates something about me rather than any feature of the situation. I say that I would find it morally impossible to stay on the terms that Lucy stayed, but how, one might ask, do I know how I would think and feel in her situation? Here I can only reply that the most we can ever do in such cases, in cases where right action is not universally determined simply by the relevant moral reasons, is *imagine* ourselves in another's place; we are not actually in their place. Sometimes that may be relatively easy, sometimes it will be harder, but imagining will never amount to *knowing* what we would decide in someone else's place. So, I *could* be mistaken in my judgement above, but that is not to say that imagining myself in Lucy's place and having to make a decision is not – despite the difficulties I have noted – the right way of attempting to understand and make a judgement about her moral decision.

Of course according to the universalizability thesis, that a moral decision is *my* decision must be irrelevant, that is, that it is me as opposed to someone else that has to make it must be irrelevant. At worst such decisions will look, on this view, like making a moral exception of oneself. But while there are certainly cases in which people do indulge in a kind of moral special pleading, it is nevertheless true that moral agency is, in a fundamental sense, personal. While we are morally accountable to others for our actions we remain, and perhaps on a more fundamental level, morally accountable to ourselves. There can be, to expand on that thought, no moral actions at all without moral agents, agents that can hold themselves capable of so acting. But if I cannot make and stand by my first-person moral judgements, then I cannot be a moral judge at all, including a judge of others. That a given course of action is not morally possible for me is a kind of bedrock of my moral identity: of what I can morally stand by and for.

In a more general way, one might say that *Disgrace* is in part about losing the capacity to make first-person moral judgements. I have touched on David's lack in this respect, but the novel also alludes to the threat of a much more widespread failure. For the events of this story take place in a post-apartheid South Africa in which white South Africans are deeply implicated in crimes just as horrific and more systemic and widespread than the one Lucy has suffered: crimes that can easily be seen to put in question a white South African's sense of their standing as a moral agent and judge. Lucy herself alludes to this when trying to understand the men who raped her: "what if *that* is the price one has to pay for staying on? Perhaps that is how they look at it; perhaps that is how I should look at it too" (*ibid.*: 158). This passage illustrates, vividly I think, the threatened sense of loss of standing in the above respect. Of course I might say, as David in fact does say to Lucy, that if these men thought that they would just be making up stories to justify themselves. But, and this is my point, *I need to be able to say it*; I need to be able to say and to believe that such "justifications" are mere rationalizations of evil, and in order to be able to say and believe that there must be, when all moral deliberation and debate has been usefully explored and exhausted, a judgement here that I can defend to myself. This much is required if one is to be a moral agent and judge at all, but there is in this case no way of expunging the "I" from one's judgement.

As others have observed, *Disgrace*, like many of Coetzee's novels, invites moral reflection in a variety of ways, and I have only touched on one aspect of such reflections here. A further aspect of *Disgrace* that I have not mentioned in this connection is the moral significance in the novel of David Lurie's altered attitude to, and relationship with, animals as the novel progresses. In terms of the ethical interest we find in *Disgrace* this is an important strand of the novel in its own right, but it is significant also, I want now to suggest, in a way that reinforces my suggestion that *Disgrace* highlights the personal nature of certain moral judgements. Reflection on our relations with animals is a significant and recurring theme in Coetzee's work,[8] and I cannot hope to provide an exhaustive account even of Coetzee's treatment of this theme in *Disgrace*. What I do want to note though is the way in which David, who initially sees our relation with animals as at best one of mere benefactor – as he says, "if we are going to be kind, let it be out of simple generosity" (*ibid.*: 74) – finally comes to register the existence of those animals he comes into contact with as making specific yet also seemingly inexplicable moral demands on him.

Nowhere are such moral demands more clearly articulated at the same time as appearing more puzzling than in David's job at an animal shelter run by Bev Shaw. Central here is David's decision to take upon himself the task of disposing of those dogs that have to be killed because there is no room for them at the shelter. Every Monday the dead dogs are taken in plastic bags to a furnace at the local hospital, with David loading the dogs on to the furnace trolley one by one. Why does David find it necessary to do this job himself? The answer is given when he describes what happens when the furnace crew do this job instead. As David tells us, stiffened with rigor mortis the dogs' legs sometimes get caught in the bars of the trolley so that the blackened corpse returns with it. David disposes of the dogs himself because "[a]fter a while the workmen began to beat the bags with the backs of their shovels before loading them, to break the rigid limbs" (*ibid.*: 144–5). What is puzzling of course is the idea that there might be a moral demand here at all: a demand that the corpses of dead dogs not be treated like this. We can understand how one might dishonour a human corpse, but these are dogs. It is a point that occurs to David himself.

> Why had he taken on this job? To lighten the burden on Bev Shaw? For that it would be enough to drop off the bags at the dump and drive away. For the sake of the dogs? But the dogs are dead; and what do dogs know of honour and dishonour anyway?
>
> For himself, then. For his idea of the world, a world in which men do not use shovels to beat corpses into more convenient shape for processing. (*Ibid.*: 145–6)

Here again we can see how moral judgement may be essentially personal. In a highly insightful discussion of this passage, Attridge makes the following claim:

> The last sentence comes as close as any in the novel to an articulation of the value that most deeply informs it ... It must be read with the previous sentence, however: this is not a practical commitment to improving the world, but a profound need to preserve the ethical integrity of the self. (2004: 187)

From a certain perspective, from the perspective that the universalizability thesis urges us to adopt, David's actions at the very end of the novel will indeed seem, as Attridge notes, "inexplicable, unjustifiable" (*ibid.*). But part of what this perspective leaves out, and what Coetzee brings to light in the above passage, is what it is to have and to live by a distinctive kind of moral idea of the world. It can make no difference to the dogs that their corpses are not beaten into a convenient shape for processing, but that is not the point. An idea of the world in which such things are not done, in which our relations with animals – even dead ones – are conditioned by a certain kind of respect *is* a distinctive moral conception of the world. Perhaps we will not share that conception; nevertheless, if someone were to say that they morally could not treat a corpse like that it would surely be a kind of perverse misunder-standing to suggest to them that really they can do this, that it is just squeamishness on their part. On the contrary, such judgements, I have argued, amount to the expression both of a particular moral idea of the world and of a particular kind of moral character.

I have focused in this chapter on one way in which moral judgement may be essentially personal and in this sense my argument here can be seen as continuous with my criticism of what might be called the prevailing view of morality and moral judgement throughout this book. Further, in advancing the argument of this chapter I have focused in particular on the importance of character in relation to moral judge-ment. However Robert Louden (1992) has argued interestingly that we might respond to the kind of sceptical challenge to morality and moral theory posed by Williams and other similar critics – and I would count myself among them – precisely by an appeal to notions of virtue or character. According to Louden, morality is "primarily … a matter of what one does or does not do to oneself rather than what one does or does not do to others" (*ibid.*: 5), and he argues that the conception of morality he develops along these lines "enables us to bridge the gulf that many antimorality critics claim exists between morality's demands and the personal point of view" (*ibid.*: 5). For Louden then, in short, "moral-ity, properly understood, *is* intensely personal" (*ibid.*: 14). But he does not think that means we need to reject morality and moral theory as its defenders commonly understand it. All the same, Louden's account of the personal nature of morality differs sharply from the position I have defended, and his attempt to characterize what he takes to be the personal dimension of morality helps to draw out what is at issue between defenders and critics of the unversalizability thesis, so I shall briefly consider Louden's argument.

Louden's strategy is to show that central features of Aristotelian and Kantian ethics are consistent with a theory of morality as essentially "self-regarding".[9] So, for example, Louden begins by focusing on Kant's idea of duties to oneself. Louden quotes approvingly Kant's claim in his *Lectures on Ethics* that:

> Far from ranking lowest, in actuality our duties to ourselves rank highest and are the most important of all for … what can

be expected of a man who dishonors himself? He who violates
a duty to himself loses his humanity and becomes incapable of
performing his duties to others.          (Quoted in *ibid*.: 13)

For Kant, of course, duty, including our duties to ourselves, springs
from the requirements of the moral law, by which Kant means *universal*
law. Still, on one way of interpreting Kant's words above – although not
one Kant would endorse – I can agree with him. For it follows from
the argument of this chapter that for a man to do what he claims he
morally cannot do really just is for him to dishonour himself. Further,
I can agree with Kant – but for the non-universalist reasons I have
given – that there is a sense in which such a person is incapable of moral
agency. So I have suggested that in order to be able to make and act on
moral judgements about others – to be a moral agent in this sense – it
is essential that one can make and defend certain first person moral
judgements to oneself. In any event, here is how Louden interprets
Kant's argument concerning duties to oneself:

> Kant's position is that without duties to oneself there could
> be no moral duties at all; for a moral duty … is by definition
> a voluntary undertaking performed from a certain specified
> motivational structure. The agent must perform the act not
> out of fear of external sticks or the hope of external carrots or
> from internal nonrational urges and impulses but rather *from
> duty*, that is, out of respect for the idea of moral law itself, as
> created by free, rational agents … The subjects of moral action
> are always self-obligating, in the sense that their own practical
> reason must move them to act. And so, at bottom, the central
> idea behind the Kantian doctrine of duties to oneself is that
> each of us has a fundamental duty to care for his or her own
> character …                                     (*Ibid*.: 15–16)

There is much in what Louden says above that I can agree with, in
particular that it is essential to morality that a person's "*own* practical
reason must move them to act" (emphasis added). My concern is, however, that Louden presents us with a false dichotomy: *either* an action
will be performed "out of fear of external sticks or the hope of external

carrots or from internal nonrational urges and impulses"; *or* it will be performed "*from duty*". But why, for example, should we suppose that if a man claims that he morally could not convict a person innocent before God, or that he could not stand by while men used "shovels to beat corpses into more convenient shape for processing", that must be *either* the expression of an impulse or urge, *or* (otherwise) a duty that just any rational agent will recognize as a requirement of the (universal) moral law? To be sure, the moral judgements that are expressed through such modalities are not universalizable, but why must we conclude that their motivational structure must be that of impulses or urges? Granted that when an agent acts on such judgements they are not acting "out of respect for the idea of moral law itself, as created by free rational agents", we can nevertheless say they are acting out of respect for *an* idea of morality – an idea of the world of the kind that Coetzee highlights in the quote above – as created by a free rational agent. What has changed here of course is our understanding of *morality* and what is involved in being a *free rational agent* and hence our understanding of the relationship between them. The argument of this book turns on our understanding morality and rational agency in ways that Louden, following Kant, may not allow (since I have rejected the universalizability thesis with respect to a class of first-person moral judgements), but that is not in itself a reason to reject the analysis I have offered. The universalizability thesis is not a *neutral* datum for moral thought and judgement let alone a condition for their very possibility. This point illustrates how the argument of this chapter is continuous with a conception of moral thought and judgement developed and defended throughout this book – and most obviously in my criticism of impartial morality in Chapter 4 – and how it may be seen to stand or fall with that conception.

## Conclusion

To return finally to my discussion of Winch, the situation that he asks us to envisage is a conflict within morality; a situation in which the various moral considerations not only do not universally determine moral judgement but actually suggest conflicting judgements. The task then is to find, even in such a situation, a moral compass, some basis upon which to decide, and that is provided, so Winch argues, by the kind of moral modalities he has highlighted. The easy reply is that there are no such dilemmas:[10] that the world is not in this way a morally conflicted place.[11] Yet, turning to my own example, a novel such as *Disgrace* may bring home to us just how morally conflicted the world can be, and how we can on that account lose our moral bearings in it. If this *is* the way the world can be, if life is sometimes like this, then one has to take seriously the kind of moral modalities I have been concerned with in this chapter, for in such situations they may be the only moral compass available to us.

# SEVEN

# Public moralism

In Chapter 3 I discussed public moralism – including by various elements of the media – in relation to art, specifically the photographic work of Bill Henson. But public moralism, including by the media, is not restricted to the moral issues raised in such cases. In this chapter I shall consider a very different kind of case: moralism about the actions of elected political leaders. To focus on the moralism that is at issue here, consider the following passage from David Owen's book *Balkan Odyssey* (1995), his account of his role as European negotiator between the warring parties in the former Yugoslavia. After sending a letter to the press and British prime minister urging military intervention to end "the morally outrageous happenings in Yugoslavia", Owen has lunch with his friend Stephen Wall, the prime minister's private secretary.

> [Stephen] explained the fears of the Chiefs of Staff of being sucked into a combatant role in what was essentially a civil war … I was being brought face to face with the harsh choices that accompany power and can be all too easily ignored by protest … Stephen … was clearly disappointed with my logic and thought I was being self-indulgent and not facing the real issues of government honestly. It was a good discipline for me, for he put me back in the Foreign Secretary's seat and did not allow me the luxury of playing to the gallery.   (*Ibid.*: 17–18)

This passage indicates a way in which there can be a kind of radical disconnect between a person's moral judgements and political reality, one that I shall suggest involves a kind of moralism. Of course there are those who argue that there is in fact a radical disconnect between morality and politics *themselves*; that morality is in a way not relevant to politics, or at least international politics such as is indicated by the example from Owen. Further, this need not be mere cynicism about politics but may be rather a considered theory about the relationship between morality and politics. For example, defenders of the theory of political realism are sceptical about the relevance of moral norms to states, or at least the relations between states. Thus political realism represents a kind of critique of morality as it is often applied to politics. The foundation for political realism can be traced to Machiavelli and Hobbes, but in the twentieth century it has included such theorists as E. H. Carr, Reinhold Niebuhr and Hans Morgenthau. It is, however, difficult to provide a definition of political realism that would be assented to by all its adherents. All the same, Tony Coady has recently provided a useful list of the central concerns of political realism that, while not perhaps common to all political realists, represent, as he says, what "Wittgenstein had in mind when he spoke of concepts that were united by overlapping strands of family resemblance" (Coady 2008: 12). These elements include, Coady goes on to suggest:

1. a certain opposition to idealism and morality in foreign affairs;
2. an opposition to moral self-inflation;
3. a concern for the national interest as a focal value for foreign policy;
4. a concern for stability in the international order;
5. a concern for close attention to the realities of power. (*Ibid.*)

The fifth concern above bears most directly on the passage from Owen I quoted above, although some of the others (notably the second concern) seem implicit in the conversation he relates. Coady himself thinks that the realists have a point in their criticisms of morality, but suggests that incompatibility between morality and politics is explained in part by a certain *moralistic* conception of morality that is here being contrasted with politics. Thus Coady suggests the real target of that realist criticism is not *morality* properly understood but *moralism*. By moralism here, Coady means a kind of vice; moreover, his way of characterizing this vice is similar to my own. Thus Coady suggests:

> we can say that the vice of moralism often involves an inappropriate set of emotions or attitudes in making or acting upon moral judgements, or in judging others in the light of moral considerations. The moralizer is typically thought to lack self-awareness and a breadth of understanding of others and of the situations in which she and they find themselves. In addition, or in consequence, the moralizer is subject to an often-delusional sense of moral superiority over those coming under his or her judgement. (*Ibid.*: 17)

While Coady goes on to divide moralism into a number of distinct types in ways I have not attempted,[1] I agree with him that the real target of realist criticism of morality in relation to politics, and particularly international politics, is best understood not as morality *per se* but moralism. My concern in this chapter is then with the way in which public protests about the actions of political leaders may be skewed by this vice.

## Politics and the problem of "dirty hands"

One way of approaching the problem of moralism about the actions of political leaders is via the so-called problem of "dirty hands" in politics. To briefly explain the idea here, there are situations in which leaders act for the good of the communities they serve, for example in trying to deal with an emergency situation, but in ways that conflict with important and deeply held moral norms. Thus it is said that in such situations leaders get their hands morally "dirty". In such situations leaders face difficult choices between what are really conflicting demands. On the one hand, there are demands that stem from some of our most deeply held moral convictions. On the other hand, and in conflict with these demands, there is demand for political action to avoid some catastrophe or even to secure the survival of the community or state the leader serves. Thus we can say that in dirty-hands-type situations, *whatever* a leader does (including nothing) will involve serious cost.

To say that whatever a leader does in a dirty-hands-type situation involves some moral cost is not, though, to say that leaders here face a genuine moral dilemma in the sense that that is understood in moral philosophy. To explain, in the case of a genuine moral dilemma, as I noted in the previous chapter (see Chapter 6, note 10), whatever an agent chooses will be morally wrong so that there is no choice that an agent may make that will be justified or necessary. In the case of dirty-hands-type conflicts, however, one choice *is* taken to be necessary even though this choice involves acting in a way that is all the same morally disagreeable. A further question related to the problem of dirty hands is then whether the conflict should be understood as a conflict *within* morality or as a conflict between morality and other values. In some cases it may make sense to say that the conflict is one within morality. Relevant here may be the kind of conflict faced by Captain Vere in Melville's *Billy Budd,* which I considered in the previous chapter. Thus Winch suggests that the enforcement of military law in relation to Billy Budd was, for Vere, a moral obligation even though Vere holds that Billy was innocent before God. Similarly we can imagine a leader holding himself *morally* obliged to defend the state they serve against internal and external threats even if that means acting in morally disagreeable ways. But it may also be that the demands of high office are often not understood most fundamentally as moral demands at all but as demands from outside morality. The question then becomes: how should we understand (and perhaps resolve) the conflict between morality and politics? I shall return to this question later in this chapter. But in order to get a clearer sense of the kind of conflict envisaged in the problem of dirty hands a further concrete example is in order.

The response of various Western democratic governments to the threat of terrorist attack in the wake of 11 September 2001 provides a striking contemporary example of the problem of dirty hands in politics.[2] So in order to meet this threat, Western governments have passed special or new legislation that involves the curtailment of many fundamental rights of citizens, including legislation for the use of preventative detention, restriction of the right to legal counsel and widened police powers including powers of search, seizure and surveillance.

There are serious moral objections one might raise to such measures, not least about whether they are *truly* necessary to combat the supposed terrorist threat. Nevertheless, it is arguable that such measures are sometimes necessary, at least in so-called cases of supreme emergency,[3] which brings me to the problem of moralism. For it can be all too easy for those of us not faced, say, with trying to balance the need for security with respect for civil liberties to caricature and condemn those who have to make such difficult compromises. To expand, it is all too easy to think of leaders in such situations as incompetent and/ or corrupt rather than as real, conscientious people in a hard place. Thus, as I argued in Chapter 2, moralism involves the caricature of others in ways that prevent us from recognizing them as aware of, and responsive to, the moral dimension of the situations they find themselves in. As I say, this is not to suggest that moral criticism of political leaders is unjustified or inappropriate, but merely to suggest that if we are not to descend into moralism here too, we need to ask ourselves honestly what someone *should do* in their situation. In particular, it is not sufficient merely to criticize some course of action actually taken; we need also to state more positively what *alternative* course of action we are recommending. What I shall argue in this chapter is that public political protest, where it is not informed by such questions or reflection, has the capacity to seriously undermine, first, public moral debate about politics and, second, active participation in democratic political processes themselves.

To begin, there is, I contend, a tendency for some journalists reporting on situations of war and other crises such as natural disasters, famine and the ongoing threat of terrorist attack, to engage in moralism as I have outlined it. Partly, as I indicated above, this can involve a moralistic caricature of those charged with responding to such crises, but it can also involve moralism in the sense, something like that touched on in Chapter 4, that we see the problems and decision leaders face in terms of a conception of morality that prevents us from seeing the full range of considerations that are properly involved in making a decision in such cases. To be clear, this is not to criticize all journalists, but to point out that the criticisms some journalists sometimes level at the actions of political leaders fail to adequately capture all that is at stake in such instances: that journalists may fail, as Owen says, "to face the real issues of government honestly". Part of the problem here, as I shall explain, is that the real issues of government are not restricted to the kinds of moral issues that feature in everyday situations of practical deliberation and choice for those of us outside high office: that sometimes political leaders are required by their institutional roles to act in ways that are questionable at best, from the point of view of such everyday moral issues.

I am not denying of course that journalists have an important role in providing moral comment on the actions of political leaders: of course they do. It is hard, for example, not to support those journalists reporting from New Orleans in the wake of Hurricane Katrina, who judged the actions of local, state and federal political leaders as shamefully inadequate. Nevertheless, the question I want to raise concerns the extent to which journalists should see themselves as moralists. Some journalists, in fact some very fine journalists, do quite openly view their role as one of moralist. So, Martin Woollacott of the *Guardian* newspaper in Britain has suggested in an article for the *Sydney Morning Herald* that foreign correspondents covering situations of war and other crises are "instinctive moralists", by which he means to compliment such journalists: his suggestion is that such journalists want to know "the rights and wrongs" of the crises they cover, that they seek to take a reflective moral view of such events (Woollacott 2005). There is much to be thankful for that there are journalists with a keen sense of, and commitment to, the demands of morality. Nevertheless a problem arises here, or so I shall argue, in so far as journalists judge the actions of political leaders in response to such crises in terms of a conception of morality that discounts many of the considerations – considerations that simply do not apply in everyday situations of practical deliberation and choice – relevant to political decision and action. Let me stress that I am not suggesting here that it is somehow inappropriate or wrong for journalists to judge, even judge very harshly, the actions of individuals in such cases. Rather, and to repeat, I am suggesting that they sometimes appeal to a conception of morality that may fail to account for all the considerations that ought properly to feature in a leader's deliberations about how to act in such cases. Thus, as I say, my argument here is related to the previous argument of Chapter 4, although it is importantly different, as we shall see later.

To expand on the above point, Woollacott sees it as an advantage of journalists that, in reporting on situations of crisis, their moral viewpoint is "distinctly autonomous, insulated to some extent from the pressures of government" (*ibid.*). In many ways this is indeed a good thing; it is certainly a good thing to have the benefit of a point of view external to actors within a crisis and be able to freely assess what is being done by those actors. Further, Woollacott is probably right in suggesting that journalists, insulated as they are from the pressures of government, find it easier to take, as he says, a "moral position" in such cases (*ibid.*). All the same, those who occupy such a viewpoint are in danger of leaving out something important in their reporting. So it is a mistake, I contend, to think that judgement of government policy or the actions of political leaders is simply a matter of determining how such policies or acts measure up to the demands of morality as we might understand them, as I say, in more everyday cases of practical deliberation and choice. What is wrong with this kind of judgement is that it counts any pressure of government that conflicts with the demands of morality so construed as somehow illegitimate: as merely distorting an agent's judgement about how they should act.

In judging the actions of a political leader in situations of crisis we need, as I have already noted, to consider the possibility that in discharging their particular role they may be required to act in certain morally disagreeable ways: that is, they may need to get their hands morally dirty. So in securing the safety of the public against acts of terrorism, for example, political leaders may, as I have suggested, find it necessary to curtail certain rights of the individual through various legislative measures: for example, rights to privacy, against detention for certain periods without charge and so on. If we were to assess such actions merely according to how they measure up to the demands of morality, as we might naturally construe them from outside the realm of political action, we may find them wanting.[4] However, this assessment of such actions misses the important point that what is morally disagreeable is sometimes required for reasons that are not visible from that perspective.

Of course there is an obvious reply one might make to the problem of dirty hands. To explain, one way of dealing with the problem is to say that here we have a situation where we face conflicting obligations, but where one of these obligations is overriding. This way of dealing with the problem more or less does away with it. So as Williams has observed, here the suggestion seems to be that "[w]hile it is not as though the ... defeated obligation had never existed ... it is quite clearly and unanswerably overridden, and complaints from the disadvantaged party would, once things had been explained, be unacceptable" (1981b: 59). In this kind of case a leader's actions are after all not morally disagreeable; what *looks* like a morally disagreeable act is in this situation completely morally acceptable, although it may still be disagreeable in some non-moral sense (e.g. psychologically hard or distasteful to perform). The kind of impartialist theories I considered in Chapter 4 would seem to respond to the problem of dirty hands in this way. Such theories propose that there really can be no problem of *morally* dirty hands; according to utilitarians, faced with two purportedly evil choices it is morally right to choose the lesser evil, while according to Kant (and his modern-day defenders) there can be no conflict of this kind since the moral law is complete and admits of no internal inconsistency.

In Chapter 4 I questioned whether such conceptions of morality make sense of the kinds of conflict between values that we sometimes face. It would be a great comfort if the kinds of difficult decisions that political leaders sometimes face could be resolved in the manner that utilitarian and Kantian theorists may suggest. However, as Williams goes on to say, not all situations of conflict are plausibly resolvable as such theories suggest; thus in some situations a sense that something discreditable has been done remains, and will, "moreover, be properly shared by the victims [so that] they will have a complaint that they have been wronged" (*ibid.*: 60). Suppose, for example, that the despotic leaders of some rogue state embark on a course of action that is not only against international law but has the effect of destabilizing neighbouring states. In such a scenario the international community may combine in applying certain sanctions targeted against the ruling elite in the offending state. But it may be that no matter how careful other nations are to avoid harming those who are innocent, the sanctions also cause suffering to the local population in a situation in which they are already suffering greatly under that regime. In the most extreme kind of case, where the rogue state acquires nuclear weapons, say, it may even be necessary to fight a war in which civilian casualties may run into hundreds or thousands or more.[5] In such scenarios, while there may be, on the one hand, compelling reasons to impose sanctions or even to go to war, it nevertheless seems perverse to suggest, on the other, that the local population has no grounds for moral complaint against the international community. But if one accepts they do have grounds for complaint then that can only be because they have been wronged; hence, the problem of dirty hands.

Of course it may be argued that while the loss of civilian life envisaged in the above scenario is morally terrible in some sense, the local population do not have grounds for complaint and so have not been wronged just in case the international community recognizes certain limits on what foreseeable but unintended killing or wounding of civilians is permitted. Perhaps some foreseeable but unintended civilian deaths in war cannot plausibly be counted as wronging civilians (the deaths of civilians unlucky enough to be at military installations when they are attacked may be an example here), but effective measures against a rogue state in the kind of worst-case scenario envisaged above may require the kind of destructive force that, even if carefully targeted, cannot but result in very significant civilian casualties. While the international community in such a case may feel that they had no choice but to use this kind of force, how political leaders characterize the actions they have taken here is important for the kind of attitude it expresses to victims and their families. Thus it seems like an evasion to me to suggest that where necessary aerial bombardment results in perhaps thousands of civilian causalities the civilian population has no grounds for complaint. Indeed, if morality or some moral theory were to discount such complaint, one might agree with Williams that we would be better off doing without such theories or morality so understood.

My suggestion is that an important part of the pressure of government just *is* the necessity to act in certain situations in ways that involve wronging particular individuals. While we may hope that a political leader may try to avoid wronging anyone, the realities involved in the exercise of real power are such that sometimes, especially in situations of crisis, there are inevitable victims – individuals who simply do not deserve to be treated as they are by government policies and decisions – and this is really part of the point Owen is making. When Owen says that his conversation with Wall put him back in the foreign secretary's seat (of course Owen was himself at one time the British foreign secretary) he is suggesting that as foreign secretary he would be bound to consider not just the "rights and wrongs" of the conflict here but also what could be done, what could be done *by us*, and how intervening or not intervening would affect vital domestic and regional interests.[6]

Let me stress that the important point above is not, say, whether or not full-scale intervention in the Balkans was justified: Woollacott, for example, suggests that the international press corps eventually reached the conclusion that it was not. Rather, the important point is that the choices here are the kinds of choices that only those who exercise real power ever have to face; that is why Owen says his conversation with Wall "put [him] back in the Foreign Secretary's seat". Most of us, including journalists, are fortunate in not having to face such choices, but we should not mistake our good fortune for some kind of advantage in assessing situations of crisis. Woollacott praises journalists for what he calls their instinct to look for the "moral high ground" (Woollacott 2005). The problem is, however, that for political leaders who have to act in situations of crisis there is often no such place: those who have to act in situations of crisis have to face the possibility that they cannot help but be morally compromised, and that the more power they wield the more compromised they are liable to become. Moreover, for a politician to assume the moral high ground in such cases is potentially dangerous or at least dishonest and unfair to those who will suffer as a result of their decisions. It is dangerous if an unwillingness to do evil has the result of bringing about what amounts to a greater evil, as a refusal to engage in strategic bombing of Germany during the Second World War might have been, for example. And it is unfair to the victims of one's action or inaction to pretend that one's hands are not morally dirty.

## Morality and politics

Of course the kind of conflict involved in the problem of dirty hands is not restricted to the field of politics. Similar kinds of conflict occur, for instance, in professional life; conflicts in this case between the moral demands of one's professional role and, again, our most deeply held moral norms. Thus, to give just one example here, a defence lawyer, as advocate, may feel obligated in virtue of their professional role to try to discredit someone they know to be a truthful witness in defending their client.[7] But the problem of dirty hands in politics may be seen to be morally problematic in a way that the conflict between occupational (or, more generally, role) morality and ordinary morality is not. That is because, as I have already noted, we may see the conflict in the former case not as a conflict between distinct moral demands at all, but simply as a conflict between morality and politics.[8] Many may then find it natural perhaps to think that in such a conflict morality should win. However, if by morality here we mean simply those deeply held moral norms that feature in what I have called everyday situations of practical deliberation and choice, we may fail to adequately represent the real issues involved in the context of political action, a context that involves considerations that do not appear in the realm of deliberation and choice that ordinary citizens, or even certain professionals, ever have to face. This way of understanding the conflict, I am suggesting, involves an inadequate, moralistic, conception of morality. We need to remind ourselves in particular that the actions of political leaders are circumscribed (and for good reasons) by the demands of their office and, more particularly, by the requirement that they act in such a way as to protect the vital interests of the state, that is, at least those interests essential to the states' continued viability. Here Williams's discussion of the particular problem of political violence is apposite. As he says:

> An important issue … is the extent to which a political leader's task, particularly in a democracy, is defined in terms of defending the interests of the state; and whether, if the interests of some other, rival, state will be advanced unless some act of violence is authorized, he can be justified in refusing to authorize that act. A similar problem arises in the case where he thinks that the interests of another state should, in justice, prevail. He certainly has the right to that opinion; to what extent has he the right to act on it while still performing that role? (Williams 1981b: 69)

It may seem that Williams is rather vague here about the relevant "interests of the state" and the kinds of acts of violence leaders may be required to authorize. Given Williams's scepticism about the capacity of moral principles and theories to resolve all practical problems, this is perhaps hardly surprising. However, there are plausible limits, first, to the relevant interests of the state and, second, to the kinds of acts of violence leaders may authorize on account of such interests. Thus, on the first point, not just any interest of the state is going to count here, although it will include at least those interests critical to the immediate survival of the state and its longer-term viability.[9] On the second point, some acts of violence, such as blatant terrorist acts on civilians of a foreign state, are likely to be ruled out simply because they undermine the very possibility of some minimum level of civil relations between rival states.

To return to the issue of the relation between our conception of morality and politics, the crucial point is just that, in assessing some crisis, our political leaders simply do not have the luxury of taking up the moral viewpoint of the international press corps. In a given situation it may be the collective moral viewpoint of the journalist of the international press corps that the interests of, say, Israel should give way to the interests of some other state or group of states. But that is not a viewpoint that the prime minister of Israel can properly take as decisive. To consider another example from Woollacott, from a viewpoint outside the actual position of the relevant political leaders, it may have been an important question to ask of the Vietnam War: "Should the United States win?" (Woollacott 2005). But that is not a question that the then United States president could legitimately have considered in deciding how to act as head of state. No head of state can legitimately hold *as head of state* that their country should simply be defeated and suffer the consequences of that defeat. In the case of war, a head of state may think it best to strategically withdraw, or sue for peace, but not simply that they should be defeated. When we consider events in war and other crises, our judgements of political leaders have to be conditioned by this kind of obvious fact.

Of course, we may think political leaders should put the interests of global justice above the interests of their own particular state. But now we are criticizing not so much the actions of particular political leaders, but the existence of the offices they hold and more generally the present world order arranged, as it is, around individual sovereign states each with the qualified right to pursue their own interests consistent with some minimum standard of respect for other states (as I alluded to above) and basic human decency. It is only reasonable to make such criticisms, but then the issue here becomes directly: how should we conceive of the conflict between morality understood as given by our most deeply held moral norms and politics, or at least international politics? Here there are at least three importantly different positions we might take. First, one could argue, in the manner I did in Chapter 4, that the scope of morality and its demands so understood is limited by certain demands that lie outside it. Thus one might argue that certain political decisions lie outside the scope of morality and that morality should have no authority with respect to them. This is a view, as Coady notes, often associated with political realism, and more or less denies the possibility of dirty hands in this context. Second, one could argue that the scope of morality so understood does extend to these political decisions but claim that it is not always possible to resolve the kinds of conflicts faced in political actions in such a way that the victims of these decisions have no grounds for moral complaint. This position simply accepts that political leaders will at times have to get their hands morally dirty. Third, one could claim that the scope of morality so understood does extend to politics and that moral considerations derived from our most deeply held moral norms always trump considerations derived specifically from politics.

To consider the third position, while it is possible to hold such a view it does not really resolve the problem of *moral* conflict. For, as I have already said, it seems implausible to suggest, given the difficult choices political leaders sometimes have to make, that there will always be an entirely morally satisfactory decision to be made. So, as I have said, while we might well choose the lesser evil, it seems odd (if not perverse) to claim the victims of that evil have no grounds for moral complaint. Moreover, such a view may lead to an unreasonable belief that the lesser evil can somehow be avoided. Thus, to insist that there is, even in the most difficult cases, some decision that a political leader might make that is not morally disagreeable seems to me to be a kind of wishful thinking. Coady suggests in this connection, for example, that "a strong moral commitment to pacifism or simply to reducing resort to war can lead to wishful thinking about the empirical political facts, as happened with the British anti-war movement's failure to appreciate the enormity of the Nazi threat in the 1930s" (2008: 27–8).

Of course a particularly tough-minded moral absolutist might argue that some kinds of actions should be morally ruled out, whatever the consequences may be. For such an absolutist the moral requirement in such cases, including cases of political action, is simply not to do evil. Consider here, for example, Elizabeth Anscombe's objection, in her pamphlet "Mr Truman's Degree", to the use of nuclear weapons on Japan at the end of the Second World War.[10] For Anscombe the central issue is that the use of these weapons involved the killing of the innocent (the civilian populations of Hiroshima and Nagasaki) as a means to end the war, and she claims that "[f]or men to choose to kill the innocent as a means to their ends is always murder" (1981: 64). The idea is that some tactics in war should be ruled out however good the consequences that come from them may be. The problem for any absolutist though, at least in the sphere of political action, is that the consequences of not performing some prohibited act can be terrible indeed, and this both puts pressure on the absolutist's doctrine and encourages wishful thinking, as Anscombe's own argument attests.

Realizing that her position will sound high-minded, she imagines the following response to her:

> Come now: if you had to choose between boiling one baby and letting some frightful disaster befall a thousand people – or a million people, if a thousand is not enough – what would you do? Are you going to strike an attitude and say "You may not do evil that good may come"? ...
>
> "It [the use of nuclear weapons on Hiroshima and Nagasaki] pretty certainly saved a huge number of lives". Given the conditions, I agree. That is to say, if those bombs had not been dropped the Allies would have had to invade Japan to achieve their aim ... Very many soldiers on both sides would have been killed; the Japanese, it is said – and it may well be true – would have massacred the prisoners of war; and large numbers

of their civilian population would have been killed by "ordinary" bombing.

... But what were the conditions? The unlimited objective, the fixation on unconditional surrender. The disregard of the fact that the Japanese were desirous of negotiating peace. The character of the Postdam Declaration – their "chance".

(*Ibid.*: 65)

I want to make two points about this passage: first, that Anscombe rather dodges the question about the boiled baby; and second, and related to this, that Anscombe's question about the conditions under which the decision to drop the bomb was made is really an evasion of the central issue. To explain, what Anscombe's appeal to the conditions here amounts to is the supposition that there was a third way to end the war; alongside the use of nuclear weapons and invasion Anscombe wants to add the prospect that something less than an unconditional surrender by the Japanese could avert the carnage of the other two options. But if that was a real option – and we might doubt that (perhaps the Japanese would have seen compromise by the Allies as a sign of weakness and fought on) – it will only be because in this case we got lucky; sometimes, and here is the problem of the boiled baby, there will be no third alternative to the proposed prohibited act and slaughter on a massive scale. The question Anscombe needs to answer, but evades, is this: are you going to let a million people perish rather than boil one baby? Or are you going to refuse to use nuclear weapons even when it is clear that the only other option will result in many more innocent people being killed? And this evasion itself looks like wishful thinking; it is as if to say that this sort of evil choice will never be realized.

Turning to the first position, it strikes me as equally implausible to claim that moral considerations, by which I mean again and in particular our most deeply held moral norms, do not even apply to many of the toughest political decisions. Whereas in Chapter 4 I suggested that there are instances when even raising moral concerns or doubts distorts our understanding of other important human values, in the case of many political decisions or acts it seems more plausible to say that moral considerations against such decisions and acts should be raised and even continue to have some force. Thus I have suggested, following Williams, that there will be times when leaders will have to act in ways that involve wronging certain individuals. So I conclude that the possibility indicated by the second position, that political leaders sometimes cannot avoid getting their hands morally dirty, is something we need to acknowledge, and that it does the media no credit if they sometimes suggest otherwise.

I am not denying that journalists have an important role to play in reporting on situations of war and other crises. Indeed, my point is to try to get clearer about what exactly that role is, or at least what it is in a democratic state. My argument here is in part that the role of journalists is not simply to convey to the public those moral issues relevant to the crisis that involve our most deeply held moral norms, but also the many political considerations – including what could be done, what could be done by us and the wider political consequences of action or inaction – that necessarily feature in the decisions of those who hold high office and have to actually act in such crises. Note, however, that this is not to suggest simply that journalists must present the point of view of politicians in such cases. What the public needs to be made aware of here is not primarily some politician's point of view – which may seem properly to require some morally disagreeable act – but the conflicting considerations that anyone who occupies that position must face and that are relevant to their decisions. That is an especially important role for a journalist where the public is that of a democratic state, because citizens play an essential part (whether they recognize this or not) in political life in such a state, which brings me to the second claim I began with, that moralism can undermine our very participation in politics.

## Politics and the challenge of participation

The reason we need journalists to be frank with us about the conflict between our most deeply held moral norms and politics, or simply the "harsh choices that accompany power", is that there is a great temptation for us to withdraw from participation in political life into protest, protest often without real commitment to change. Here is an example of what I mean. Years ago I was stuck in rush-hour traffic in Sydney and in front of me was a brand new luxury four-wheel-drive vehicle (an SUV). In the back window of the vehicle the owner had placed the following message in large print on a piece of paper: "No war for oil". This was during the time of the Second Gulf War (or the Iraq War of 2003) and such sentiments were not uncommon. The message implied by the protest seemed to be that the war was somehow being fought in part to secure supplies of oil to Western countries (like Australia): that it was being fought to secure economic interests, the interests that support the current way of living. But I wondered at the time (and still do) just how serious the owner of this expensive gas-guzzling symbol of lifestyle was in making this protest.

I do not intend to enter into the debate about whether the Second Gulf War was really fought for oil, or whether if we had not fought the war that would have had any effect on the supply of oil. Be that as it may, what the person making the protest must at least have meant is something like this: I morally object to this war, which is being fought to secure oil supplies to the West. So, we might think they must have been prepared to accept the consequences *as they saw it* of not fighting this war: that the supply of oil to the West may be reduced or interrupted, so they are prepared to find alternative means of transport and even are willing to accept a significant financial write-off on their brand new vehicle. Pollyanna would certainly think so. I, however, have my doubts. I have suggested several times already, in Chapters 3 and 5 explicitly, that moral judgement can seem easy but that serious moral reflection and judgement is actually often very difficult, and that the moralizer here takes the easy road (pardon the pun) of judging others while themselves failing the test of serious moral reflection, including reflection on their own behaviour. It is of course possible (who can say?) that the owner of the vehicle in my example was indeed deeply committed to the views they were expressing (perhaps they were on the way back to the car salesroom to trade the vehicle in). Nevertheless, I think one *would be* a kind of Pollyanna if one were not to look more critically at this kind of public moral protest.

The perception of political impotence, my example suggests, has its benefits. If change is out of my hands I can defer action, perhaps defer selling the SUV, until change is somehow brought about by those who do have it in their power.[11] What I can do, all I can do, is protest and declare my allegiance with others who protest in like manner, including many in the media. The perception of political impotence combined with the satisfaction of protest can lead to a general disengagement with politics or political debate. In bringing the tension between politics and our moral norms to the attention of the public, journalists in a democratic society can serve the crucial function of encouraging citizens to ask themselves some of the most important questions about the kind of government they should have, questions basically about the proper limits of the state's power in pursuing its own vital or even merely strategic interests. And as citizens of a democratic state, it is their *responsibility* to ask themselves such questions. Specific questions include, for example, what particular interests of the state warrant going to war, or how aggressively should one state (say, a First World state) pursue its own trade interests where this may adversely affect the interests of another (say, poor Third World) state? The view from some supposed moral high ground is not very helpful in answering such questions, since the answer to such questions – which may involve balancing the qualified[12] rights of states to pursue their own interests with broader more universal demands of justice – may remain morally disagreeable in ways that those who assume the moral high ground are loath to accept. Indeed, the moral high ground is, I am suggesting, a kind of self-indulgent illusion: as Owen says, an "avoidance of the real issues of government". And journalists fail us, and indeed their own commitment to reporting the truth, in so far as they seek it.

## Idealism

It could be said that throughout this book there has been a strong current of scepticism. By this I do not mean philosophical scepticism, that is to say, scepticism as a method of doubt to determine what we know, or to find a firm foundation for knowledge, but a more everyday scepticism about the specific claims people make. In particular my arguments have involved a scepticism or doubt about whether people's moral judgements are always what they claim to be: that is, a serious and reflective attempt at moral thought, as opposed to mere moralism.

But at this point, and particularly given the above discussion about political participation, I want to dispel any idea that this scepticism, or perhaps wariness, about the moral judgements of others must lead to a kind of despair or a fatalistic acceptance of the world as it is. It is true that in reflecting on political action, especially in a crisis, we need to be aware, as we might say, of the political realities on the ground. But political realism in this limited sense does not stand opposed to something else that, I now want to suggest, is also important in moral and political thought, that is, idealism.

By idealism I mean to point to the place of certain ideals in human life. One feature of ideals of course is that they are not limited to morality or politics but span all significant human values. Thus an artist can aspire to realize certain aesthetic ideals in her work. Another feature of ideals, which the last sentence already highlights, is that there is a sense in which it is often said that ideals are unrealizable. The ideal is, some might say, always beyond our human endeavours. Interestingly, in the case of art at least, such unrealizability does not usually lead to any kind of despair for the artist but is often a spur to greater artistic achievement in an attempt to approach the ideal more closely. How, in this respect, one can even aim at the ideal if it is unrealizable is a puzzle I do not intend to grapple with here. What is important for my purposes is just that somehow we can be guided by ideals; that we can pursue them in our life and work; that it does not follow from their unrealizability (if that is indeed so[13]) that we must give up in despair.

As with artistic ideals so with other ideals, such as the moral ideal of justice; the mere fact that perfect justice may not be practically realizable in the world as it is here and now need not lead us to despair or a weary acceptance of the status quo. That can happen of course, and there are people who scoff at genuine moral commitments and idealism. But an equal threat to political action in modern liberal democracies is mistaking moralism for idealism. Idealism is not the same thing as idle protest or wishful thinking, so believing that people can change their way of thinking and acting is not just wishful thinking because sometimes they do. Many successful struggles against injustice testify to this fact, including the abolition of slavery and, more recently, the end of racial segregation in, for example, the United States and South Africa. Those who defended the ideal of justice in such cases were not wrong-headed or unrealistic let alone moralistic. To consider a current issue, as I write it looks as if the prospects of the global community of nations reaching a binding agreement to meet the challenge of man-made global warming are depressingly slim. But they are not zero and there are things within the power of ordinary citizens in developed and developing nations that can make meaningful action more likely.

A further confusion about ideals in relation to morality and politics though is the distinction between being committed to the ideal of justice and being unwilling in practice to accept anything other than the ideal. So those for whom only the perfectly just outcome is acceptable are guilty of moralism in the sense I have characterized it; in their case moral thought and reflection may be distorted by a failure to recognize, as Owen puts it, "the harsh choices that accompany power". Of course, in the case of some people who stick to an ideal in the face of the political and other realities, matters may appear more complicated. Thus well-meaning and otherwise morally thoughtful people sometimes pursue admittedly important moral ideals, although in situations in which those ideals are not only practically unrealizable but where the wholehearted pursuit of these ideals ends up making matters worse. Government policy in Australia related to its Indigenous peoples is arguably littered with misplaced idealism of this sort. Thus, for example, the prominent Indigenous leader Noel Pearson has argued that "when you really analyse the nostrums of progressive policy, you find that the pursuit of these policies has never helped us to resolve our problems – indeed they have only made our situation worse" (Pearson 2000).[14] Much of what Pearson calls "progressive policy" here has been aimed at the preservation of the language and culture of specific Aboriginal and Torres Strait Island groups, particularly in remote Indigenous communities: certainly a laudable ideal as Pearson himself believes. But the practical obstacles to creating what ideally amounts to a kind of nation (or nations) within a nation are enormous and the reality is now that many of the remote communities that were supposed to be the custodians of Indigenous languages and culture are ghettos of welfare dependency with horrific problems of alcoholism, substance abuse and even child abuse.

To consider a smaller and more personal example of the kind of misplaced idealism I have just noted, in many Australian universities there are dedicated Indigenous learning centres where Indigenous students can meet and study together. Presumably similar ideals to do with preserving Indigenous culture are in play here.[15] But such centres, while laudable in many ways, can have unexpected and disastrous side effects for some students. I once received an essay from an Aboriginal first-year student in which he had confused Descartes' "dreaming argument", essentially to do with the certain foundation of our knowledge, with the Aboriginal "dreamtime". This student had spent all his time with students in the Indigenous learning centre and had had no communication with other philosophy students in the mainstream student body. This is not to deny that first-year students from all sorts of backgrounds miss the point of Descartes' argument in fundamental ways; philosophy is a hard subject. But this error seemed of an entirely different order, and one that could have been avoided if this student had had even a casual conversation with some of his philosophy classmates.

It might seem odd (even unfair) to say that those responsible for well-meant but failed policies, for example about Indigenous affairs, are guilty of moralism, especially if they do not assume some kind of moral high ground or condemn others for failing to pursue the ideal. Nevertheless such cases still involve a failure to think seriously enough about how we ought to act in the real practical situations we face, although I concede that in such cases our response to such misplaced idealism may properly be quite complex. Thus on the one hand it seems right to admire the kind of commitment that some people display in even the unrealistic pursuit of important moral ideals, but on the other hand it seems right also to deplore some of the same people's lack of hard thinking about the gap between the reality and the ideal. I was struck by an example of this kind of failure on a more trivial level reading a newspaper article in the aftermath of Hurricane Katrina. The actor Sean Penn had travelled to a flooded New Orleans to help in the rescue effort. One might grant Penn's moral commitment or idealism, but all the same he did not appear to think through even the most basic practicalities of his plan. Thus he had neglected to put the stopper in the bottom of his small rescue boat, which promptly began to sink so that he was soon in need of rescue himself.

## Conclusion

I have argued that our most deeply held moral norms do still apply to the actions of political leaders and to international politics. However, I have also argued that such moral considerations are not the only considerations, nor necessarily the decisive considerations, in assessing the actions of political leaders on the international stage. What serious moral thought or reflection requires of us in this context is an understanding of the limits of morality so construed in relation to politics. In Chapter 4 I argued against a conception of morality as playing a kind of adjudicating role in relation to all other values that may feature in our various practical deliberations. Such a conception I argued there, and in a different connection have argued in this chapter, provides a distorted picture of what certain situations of practical deliberation and choice are really like. Thus on this picture there is the idea that if only we were to allow morality this adjudicating role in relation to international politics, then once morality has passed judgement there is nothing more to be said. More specifically, this is to say that there is nothing that remains to be said in favour of those considerations that are defeated or in complaint by those who suffer harm because of that judgement. Or, in other words, this is to say, in terms of the metaphor of "dirty hands", that our hands are clean, which is to say that our conscience is clear. My contention has been, first, that life is just not like that: that in terms of the crises and conflicts political leaders sometimes face there just is no such moral position or high ground. But also, second, that in so far as we continue to assume just this kind of high ground in relation to our judgement of the actions of political leaders, serious debate on the issues is foregone and any serious participation in the political processes by us is undermined. Thus once again I have argued that moralism, here in relation to our judgement of political leaders, undermines serious moral reflection and judgement

# Conclusion

While I have had an interest in exploring the nature of moralism as a vice for some time, the main catalyst for writing this book was the moral furore over the exhibition of Australian artist Bill Henson discussed above. But at the time the driving force for me was not most prominently a concern to explore, as I do in Chapter 3, the possible significance of art to moral thought and reflection; on the contrary, what drove me was really my own moral response to these events, a response not most directly to Henson's images but to the way in which the girl in the offending image along with her family were treated by many of those who objected most strongly to them. What struck me about many of those moral objections and judgements, as I shall explain below, was a certain lack of fellow feeling for the girl and her family. What the Henson case seemed to me to illustrate in a fairly striking way is how much more moral thought or reflection requires of us than simply making moral judgements, and how a failure to appreciate this results in moral judgement being nothing more than moralizing. Moralism, I have suggested, is a vice that involves a failure to recognize what moral thought or reflection requires (and does not require) of us in this broad sense. And this book is an attempt to more fully articulate this idea so as to better understand the proper nature of moral thought, reflection and judgement. But the moral furore over Henson may also serve to help summarize many of the central arguments of this book, so I return

153

now to the Henson case, but this time to a televised debate in which many of those who featured in the public controversy were involved, including Hetty Johnston.

Johnston, a vocal campaigner against child abuse, was on record before the televised debate took place as suggesting that Henson's images, including the image of the twelve-year-old girl at the centre of the controversy, were clearly pornographic and she wanted the police "to prosecute, both the gallery and the photographer, but I'd like to see the parents as well looked into" (reported in Tovey *et al.* 2008). Consider the following extract from the transcript of that debate reproduced by David Marr in his book on the Henson case:

> "How is the girl going to feel," asked a member of the SBS *Insight* audience that night [herself a teenage girl], "when she has to hear all these sorts of things said about a photograph of her?"
>
> "Well I didn't take a photograph of her and stick it out there – Bill Henson did," replied Johnston. "So if anyone's got to answer for that it's Bill Henson, not me and certainly not the Prime Minister."
>
> "You were the one who pointed the finger," interjected the photographer Sandy Edwards. "You have to take responsibility for that, Hetty. You have to."
>
> "I am not shirking anything I've done. I am simply saying to you I would not have seen the photo and I wouldn't have made a comment on it if Bill Henson hadn't've taken it."
>
> (Marr 2008: 72)

This exchange, it seems to me, invites the question: what, in the case of our moral thought and judgement, are we exactly responsible for? One answer to that question (an answer that I have suggested is deficient) is that we have a responsibility to ensure to the best of our ability that our moral judgements are true. But a more adequate answer to this question requires a clear sense of the further kinds of demand moral thought and judgement make of us. What the above exchange demonstrates, I think, is some of the different ways in which we might fail, as I have argued, to appreciate these further demands.

To begin, consider the question the young girl asks of the *Insight* audience: "How is she going to feel ... when she hears all these sorts of things said about a photograph of her?" What sort of response does it require? If we think that Henson's images are in fact morally problematic, then we might also think, as perhaps Johnston does, that it requires no direct response at all. Here it is important to note that the girl who asks this question is not herself making a judgement about Henson's images or more generally about the ethics of photographing naked minors; she is not making a judgement at all. But then if one thinks there are moral concerns with Henson's images, what can be the objection to raising them or making a judgement about them? To put the point more bluntly, what can a girl's feelings about what is said about a photo of her have to do with it? What the girl's feelings have to do with it, I suggest, is that they should matter to us, that they should move us and that our judgements should be informed by our being so moved. What the question requires then is not a judgement but something quite different. I have argued in Chapter 2 that morality requires of us something more than making correct or at least defensible moral judgements. What may seem lacking in Johnston's response is perhaps a certain sympathy or concern for those who are impacted by the whole affair and particularly by her own moral judgements. One particular reason we might think this kind of response is especially important here is that it is after all out of concern for the girl in the photograph, or at least minors generally, that these objections to Henson were even raised. So in response to the question "How is the girl going to feel?", what is required perhaps is simply some expression of sympathy or compassion for the girl in the photograph and perhaps also for her parents. Even if one remains convinced that Henson's images are morally problematic that, the thought is, is not all that matters.

I argued in Chapter 2 that our immediate emotional responses to others, as distinct from our judgement of them, can be a form of recognition of their humanity and that moral judgement divorced from such responsiveness is a kind of hollow sham. But it is also important to note that this kind of responsiveness is essentially personal; what is at issue here is a kind of emotional responsiveness through which one particular human being recognizes the humanity of another particular human being. This is why it is important that the girl's question, considered in the last paragraph, is directed to each of us. What the above exchange makes plain is that such an address can be hard to face and very tempting to try to dodge. So it is telling perhaps that, when challenged to take responsibility for "pointing the finger", Johnston says, "I would not have seen the photo and wouldn't have made the comment on it if Bill Henson hadn't've taken it". Johnston presents events merely as a case of cause and effect and what is left out is that she chose to make her comment. This is not to deny that she has a right to comment but merely to point out that this way of putting it removes her from the picture entirely. Another kind of demand that morality makes on us then, as I discussed in Chapter 6, is that we are able to stand by and for the moral judgements we make. A test, sometimes the hardest test, of our capacity to stand by and for our judgements is the ability to face those whom our judgement is directed against without deflection or excuse. There is an even more striking example of the failure to do this in the debate on *Insight* to which I have been referring. Earlier in the programme viewers heard the story of artist Concetta Petrillo. Concetta, or Connie, was charged with indecently recording a child under the age of thirteen when she produced naked and semi-naked photographic images of her children for an assignment within an art course. Connie was not ultimately convicted of this offence but when asked directly by the debate moderator whether Connie, who was in the audience, should have been prosecuted, Johnston could not bring herself to say yes, even though those photographs must have been pornographic too if Henson's images were. Obviously that would have been a hard thing to say directly to someone. But if a person truly believes in their judgement to that effect they ought to be able to pronounce it, and if they cannot or are unwilling to pronounce it we might wonder whether they have really reflected enough – and in the kinds of ways I have outlined in this book – on their judgement.

The spirit of the point above is intended, although perhaps it does not immediately appear so, to be more optimistic than critical. I count it as a point in Johnston's favour that, in spite of her moral objections to children being photographed naked for public display, she drew back when faced with the prospect of simply condemning Connie, to her face, for taking such photographs. This may seem strange, for Johnston had earlier said to the press that she wanted the parents of the girl in

Henson's photograph "looked into" by the police. Where now is the courage of her convictions? Well, and here is my optimism, hearing Connie's story we might think that Johnston's judgment was tempered by sympathy, pity or by what in Chapter 2 and more generally I have called a kind of "fellow feeling". Such responses – to be moved in these primitive ways (as I have called them) by the presence of another human being – are, I have argued, more basic in us than our sense of a requirement to judge. My point is not to condemn Johnston: far from it. Rather it is, first, to point out again that moral thought and reflection involve more, demand more from us, than merely making moral judgements and, second, to suggest that the kinds of responses that are required of us are, anyway, there in the background and that they sometimes, more than anything else, prevent moral judgement and debate descending into an ugly exercise in finger-pointing.

I said above that this book is about understanding the kinds of demands that moral thought and judgement make on us. But part of the problem here is also, as discussed in Chapter 4, recognizing the limits to morality and its demands in human life. One way in which our moral thought and judgement can be flawed is by their overreaching their proper bounds. Thus there is the tendency, as I have argued, for morality to play an overweening role in human life, a tendency that can have disastrous consequences. Consider finally what I take to be the cautionary tale of Prince Myshkin in Fyodor Dostoyevsky's *The Idiot* (Dostoyevsky [1868] 2004). Prince Myshkin, or "Prince" as he is called, actually embodies a number of the kinds of moralistic failings I have been concerned with in this book. The problem with the prince is not merely that with him morality overreaches its proper bounds, but also that the way in which he pursues the moral path is strangely emotionally empty and so, in a way, blind. Indeed, the prince illustrates how a tendency for morality to overween in a person's life and a lack in the same life of the kind of emotional responsiveness I have suggested is so essential to our understanding of others and the situations we face can work in unison. The prince, we immediately recognize, is a kind of innocent; suffering from epilepsy, which earns him the appellation "idiot", he has spent much of his young life in relative isolation away from society and his homeland, Russia. On his return to St Petersburg it is clear that he is humble, compassionate, always assuming the best of others and immediately forgiving them their transgressions even as they exploit him for their own gain. For it is also clear that the society to which the prince has returned is deeply corrupt. In short his is a saint-like character surrounded on all sides by vain, selfish narcissists and scoundrels. All the same, by the end of the novel we can perhaps begin to see, as Susan Wolf has suggested, why someone might "regard the absence of moral saints in their life as a blessing" (1982: 421); for the prince's extreme, even saintly, goodness turns out to be disastrous for those closest to him.

On his return to Russia, the prince is loved by, and in different ways himself loves, two women. First, and after only seeing her photograph, he loves Nastasya Filippovna, a great beauty who as a child had been groomed by her guardian Totsky to be his young concubine. But the prince is not entranced by Nastasya's beauty so much as by the suffering he detects in her face, suffering caused by the violation of her innocence by Totsky. So the prince loves her out of compassion for what she has endured. Determined to save Nastasya from a disastrous marriage to the passionate but also violent Rogozhin, the prince offers to marry her. But Nastasya, although she loves the prince, runs away from him, unwilling to let him sacrifice himself for her sake. Later the prince falls in love with Aglaya Ivanovna, the youngest and still immature daughter of Lizaveta Prokofyevna, a supposed distant relation to the prince. Not wanting the prince to ruin his life through his compassionate love for her, Nastasya eventually tries to promote his marriage instead to Aglaya. But Aglaya is young, inexperienced and consequently madly jealous of the older and more sophisticated Nastasya, and so drags the prince along with her to see Nastasya so as to reassure herself that the prince loves her more than her rival. Nastasya, although she knows she can compel the prince to marry her, is prepared to give him up to Aglaya. But Aglaya's hatred for her during their meeting is so intense that something in Nastasya snaps and she declares hysterically that she could command the prince to marry her if she wished. As both women stare at the prince in expectation, he is silent until he can endure the sight of Nastasya's suffering no further and pleads to Aglaya "How can you do this? I mean, she is … so unhappy!" (Dostoyevsky [1868] 2004: 666). The prince, seeing how much suffering these words have caused Aglaya, eventually goes to her, but his momentary hesitation is too much for the young girl to bear and she rushes from the room humiliated.

At this stage at the end of the novel the narrator has given up any attempt to interpret events and this tasks falls to Yevgeny Pavolvich, who is a friend of Aglaya's family and her one-time suitor. In this affair, as Yevgeny sees it, the prince has mistaken, particularly in the case of Nastasya, "an enormous, rushing mass of cerebral convictions ... for genuine, natural and spontaneous convictions". Turning specifically to the meeting between Nastasya and Aglaya, Yevgeny goes on:

> But for the sake of compassion ... was it justifiable to disgrace another girl, one who was high-minded and pure, to degrade her in those [Nastasya's] arrogant, those hate-filled eyes? But to what lengths will compassion take you after that? ... And I mean, you did make her a proposal, you made it to her in front of her parents and her sisters!
>
> ... And where then was your heart, that "Christian" heart of yours? I mean, you saw her face at that moment: well, was she suffering less than the *other*, than *your* other, her rival in love? How could you see that and allow it? How?      (*Ibid*.: 677–8)

Distraught, the prince pleads with Yevgeny to go with him to Aglaya, insisting that Aglaya will understand. To which Yevgeny replies, "No, Prince, she won't understand! Aglaya Ivanovna loved like a woman, like a human being, and not like ... an abstract spirit. Do you know what, my poor Prince? It's highly likely that you never loved either the one or the other!" (*ibid*.: 680).

The prince's compassion or love, if one can call it that, is an abstract inhuman kind of love. While he claims the he will die without Aglaya, it is hard to believe him. The prince's convictions, as Yevgeny notes, are "cerebral" rather than "genuine, natural and spontaneous". For all his abstract compassion for Nastasya, the prince lacks the kind of primitive emotional responsiveness to particular human beings that I have argued is essential to understanding others and what a given situation demands of us. The prince loves with a kind of equanimity, but nobody in an intimate or even personal human relationship expects to be loved like that. As Yevgeny also says, "You will agree, Prince, that in your relations with Nastasya Filippovna there was from the very outset something *conventionally democratic*" (*ibid.*: 676). One can imagine, as Yevgeny does, what the prince must have been thinking faced with these two women who loved him so; we can imagine him being morally torn between the different but equally pressing need of both women at that moment. But that is what is so terrible about this scene; love cannot, will not, be weighed like that in some kind of moral scales. This is why Yevgeny wonders whether the prince truly loved either of them. Even after listening to all Yevgeny has to say the prince still does not really see the point. He merely repeats again and again that he is "to blame" for it all. But that is not the crucial point. What exasperates Yevgeny is that in the stand-off between Nastasya and Aglaya the prince does not see that what was required of him was not some kind of judgement – say, about whose suffering was the greatest – but an immediate, what I have called primitive, *response*. What Yevgeny does not understand is the prince's *hesitation*. If the prince really loved Aglaya in the way that he claims, then he should not have had to think about what to do; he would, rather, have rushed to her immediately and without thinking. The prince's failure to do this indicates a fundamental failure to understand what human life is like and the kinds of demands it makes on us. The prince is undoubtedly extremely morally thoughtful, selfless and in a generalized way compassionate, but at the same time he thinks too much about morality (and about things one should not have to think about), he is too selfless, and his compassion is too general, and for these reasons he is in the end truly a kind of idiot.

To be clear, my point is not most fundamentally to agree with the prince that he is "to blame"; that, frankly, lets him off too lightly. Indeed, to describe Yevgeny's indignation as *moral* indignation can seem too weak. Moral ideas or concepts, mere moral ideas or concepts I should like to say, hardly capture a sense of what the prince lacks, of what is missing in his relations to other human beings. It is a challenge, a creative challenge, finding the words to explain what the prince lacks. But we get perhaps a sense of it earlier in the novel when the prince informs Aglaya that the consumptive boy, Ippolit, has tried to kill himself. Ippolit has read a written "confession" to the prince and a group of his friends and associates before trying unsuccessfully to shoot himself, a confession that he wants delivered to Aglaya, with whom he is infatuated. As the prince relates it, Ippolit "probably wanted us all to surround him and tell him that we love and respect him very much, and wanted us to implore him to remain alive" (*ibid.*: 497). When Aglaya says that she understands what Ippolit had in mind, that when she was younger she had thought of poisoning herself, writing a letter about it, and imagining her parents weeping over her coffin, the prince smiles, then laughs. To which Aglaya replies:

> I really don't feel like joking with you ... I will see Ippolit; please let him know. But as for you, I think you behave very badly, because it's very ill-mannered to examine and judge a man's soul in the way that you judge Ippolit. You have no tenderness: only truth, and so you're not fair.     (*Ibid.*: 497–8)

For all his goodness, and despite the fact that what he says about the boy is perfectly true, there is something quite chilling in the matter-of-fact way the prince talks about Ippolit. Aglaya is right; the prince is not being "fair". But in what sense is he not being fair? If in trying to make sense of this thought we restrict ourselves merely to just those moral ideas or concepts considered licit in much contemporary analytic philosophy – impartiality, objective interests, welfare and obligation, to name but a few – it is difficult to see how we can explain it. We need other resources to account for it, not least emotional resources. This book is an attempt, really only the beginning of an attempt, to explain what those resources might be. So how then is truth without tenderness not fair? It is not fair because what others may properly demand of us is that they – their life, their plight – should move us in ways that do not depend on and are not ultimately subject to the findings of moral theories, principles and judgements: that we are moved towards them, for example, out of pity, sympathy, friendship, tenderness.

# Notes

## 1. Moralism and related vices

1. Of course I do not deny that there will be cases where the *refusal* to morally judge – say, to speak out against grave injustice – is unreasonable, even wrong. That opposite tendency is common enough and I do not wish to discount it. It is not, though, the subject of this book.
2. Note that one might in contrast engage in moral thought, reflection or judgement reluctantly, with sorrow even. This is a theme I shall explore in Chapter 2.
3. Note that it may be argued, as for example does Julia Driver (2006), that moralism is always directed at judging others, that there is no kind of internal moralism. On this point I disagree with Driver, as will become clear later.
4. Devlin opposed the conclusion of the Wolfenden Report, arguing that there is a role for the enforcement of morals by law, whereas Hart argued against Devlin's legal moralism. For Hart's response to Devlin at the time, see his "Immorality and Treason" ([1959] 1993). For extended accounts of both arguments, see Devlin (1965) and Hart (1963).
5. An exponent of the view he calls "ethicism" – that moral defects in a work of art are always aesthetic defects and that (aesthetically relevant) moral merits are always aesthetic merits – is Berys Gaut; see Gaut (2007). For the more moderate view that sometimes moral defects/merits are aesthetic defects/merits, see Carroll (1996).
6. For Williams's account of the "morality system", see in particular his *Ethics and the Limits of Philosophy* (1985).
7. I say here that the conflict between public judgement and private conduct must involve the hypocrite in an element of pretence in order to handle some

obvious counter-examples. A continuing drug addict, for example, might claim that one ought not to use drugs, so their public pronouncements are in conflict with their actual conduct, but there need be no pretence so the addict is not a hypocrite. There would only be pretence if they were at the same time presenting themselves as something they are not, as would be the case if they hid their addiction.

8. This is not to suggest that all those who defended Henson were themselves without fault. Thus, for someone to call any moral concern with Henson's images mere philistinism perhaps expresses a comparable vice to moralism within the field of aesthetics. So just as the moralizer can inappropriately make moral judgement about art, thus discounting aesthetic values, so some particularly one-eyed defenders of art can make blanket aesthetic judgements about what are appropriately moral matters, thus discounting important moral values. Further, if someone were to frame their defence of Henson's images in terms of the *moral* rights of artist, then they too could be guilty of moralism.

9. Here I have been greatly influenced in particular by Alice Crary's *Beyond Moral Judgment* (2007).

## 2. *The Scarlet Letter*: "a tale of human frailty and sorrow"

1. The quote in the chapter heading is taken from Nathaniel Hawthorne's *The Scarlet Letter* ([1850] 1960: 50).

2. It might be said that, at least sometimes, moralism involves not a lack of responsiveness to others but the wrong kind of responsiveness, say, an eagerness to find fault in others. While I do not deny this, what I want to argue is that what is most basic in the kind of case that concerns me in this chapter is a lack of responsiveness to another that involves a failure to recognize the other's humanity. Thus, on my understanding of these cases, an eagerness to find fault with another is itself explained by the moralizer's failure to recognize that the person judged already both recognizes the full moral significance of their fault and holds themselves accountable for it. But to consider a different kind of case, an eagerness to find fault with another may otherwise be explained by a desire to humiliate or dominate them. However, such a tendency, while also a vice, seems quite distinct from moralism.

3. Concerning pity, it is worth noting that sometimes this term is used with an accent of condescension or disrespect; for example, when a good-looking, popular girl says to her more homely classmate, "What a shame it is about your nose". However, this strikes me as a derivate use of a term whose most basic meaning is morally positive. For a discussion of pity intended as disrespect or condescension, see Tudor (2000).

4. Winch raises this point in connection with his interpretation of Wittgenstein's remarks concerning "An attitude towards a soul" in part two of Wittgenstein's

*Philosophical Investigations.* The following argument is greatly influenced by Winch's interpretation of Wittgenstein. For an extended account of the argument presented below, see my *Sympathy: A Philosophical Analysis* (2002).

5. For a recent and useful related discussion, see Read (2010).

6. As I understand it, sympathy is distinct from pity. While sympathy involves being moved to help another who is suffering, pity is a response to the suffering of another where there is no possibility of helping the sufferer. Thus the chorus in Sophocles' *Oedipus Rex* can only pity Oedipus' plight because they cannot help him.

7. I will consider just such a case in Chapter 5. A relevant source of doubt about a person's recognition of some wrong they have done may be our belief that they are perpetuating it. I thank Rupert Read for bringing this point to my attention. I do not agree with him, however, that Dimmesdale's inability to admit his guilt contributes to Hester's misery or perpetuates injustice. Hester herself, for example, is not prepared to expose Dimmesdale because of her continuing feelings for him.

8. It could be objected that the opposite of caricature, the kind of idealization of a person that occurs in hagiography, likewise involves a failure to present a person as a real human being. However, while hagiography is not offensive in quite the same way as moralism, we might equally say that we owe it to the great and the good not to reduce them, if not to caricatures then to mere ciphers. But to consider a different point, we should not confuse merely taking someone to exemplify some moral ideal or virtue with idealizing that person's life. For example, we can hold up Nelson Mandela as exemplifying virtues such as courage and integrity without in any way detracting from our sense of the man as a real human being.

9. I thank Antony Duff for bringing this point to my attention.

10. This is not to say that Dimmesdale would be forgiven by many in his own congregation. But even in a community such as this, understanding and forgiveness are possible, as the scene with Hester at the pillory that I have related suggests.

11. I thank Andrew Gleeson for helping to clarify this point.

12. This is a point I shall return to in Chapter 5.

13. Consider, for example, the version of moral cognitivism advanced by Jonathan Dancy in his *Moral Reasons* (1993). A similar point can perhaps be made about John McDowell's arguments in various papers identifying virtue with knowledge, including his: "Virtue and Reason" (1979) and "Are Moral Requirements Hypothetical Imperatives?" (1978).

14. Again, this is not to say that questions of justification cannot come up on some occasions. My point is that these cases, cases where, say, our pity for another appears to stand in need of justification, are really unusual cases: cases that exist against a background of responsiveness to others, where such questions or doubts do not come up. For example, there will be cases where there is some

reason to doubt that a person is suffering in a *particular* way, where there is a doubt, for example, about whether a person is really suffering the pangs of remorse as opposed to the pain of lost reputation.

15. For an account of this affair, see Marr & Wilkinson (2004).
16. In thinking this, I have been deeply influenced by the work of Raimond Gaita. See in particular his *Good and Evil* (1991) and *A Common Humanity* (1998).


## 3. Trusting oneself

1. The Roslyn Oxley9 Gallery website is www.roslynoxley9.com.au/artists/18/ Bill_Henson/ (accessed October 2011). At the time of writing the image on the Henson 2008 exhibition invitation is no longer posted, although some of the other controversial images of adolescents remain.
2. For an extended account of the controversy over Henson, see *The Henson Case* by David Marr (2008). While Marr is not exactly an impartial observer – he is firmly in Henson's corner – he does nonetheless faithfully record all the important events surrounding the controversy. The book also reproduces the nude image that produced the initial moral outrage.
3. This is an issue that I shall return to, and examine in some detail, in Chapter 5.
4. I am not saying of course that it *necessarily* follows from the fact that a public figure, a politician, say, calls Henson's image "revolting" that they are guilty of moralism. In the case of a given politician it may be that they *do reflect privately* on their response to such an image, but that they are not prepared to accept the potential damage to their career of airing such thoughts or reflections *publicly*. While such a person may not be guilty of moralism, in so far as there is a conflict in their case between their public claims and private convictions, they could reasonably be charged with the related vice of hypocrisy (see my discussion on hypocrisy in Chapter 1). Concerning such hypocrisy, though, there may be sound political reasons on at least some occasions for an elected politician to be less than entirely honest about their private convictions, for example, where the potential damage to their reputation will undermine their ability to stay in power so to achieve important social change. I thank Rupert Read for reminding me of this general point. I shall examine the relationship between politics and morality in some detail in Chapter 7.
5. I say we would be wise to be suspicious. To be clear, this is not to condemn anyone. It is merely to suggest that to use such extreme and morally charged language to describe an image that was in the end rated PG, or (as might have happened in this case) to use such language in condemning the mere idea of art taking this kind of subject matter (adolescent sexuality), surely invites certain moral questions.
6. For an account on the censorship of obscenity in the arts in Australia,

including the Ern Malley trial, see Coleman (1974). For an extended account of the whole Ern Malley affair, see Heyward (1993).

7. One might argue that there is little agreement about what makes for an obscene or pornographic image. But the task of the Australian Classification Board would be impossible if there were not some consensus on these matters. And, as I have noted, this board has classified PG the image by Henson at the centre of this controversy.

8. One might go so far as to say that children cannot consent to be photographed in any way for public display and that it is the responsibility of parents to protect their children from the public gaze much more generally.

9. On this point it was striking that at the time of the original controversy about Henson, and subsequently when I have presented earlier versions of the argument of this chapter, many people have felt able to judge that Henson ought not to be allowed to take these kinds of photographs of children *without actually ever having seen the photographs in question.*

10. It is interesting that these earlier images did not create the kind of furore surrounding Henson's 2008 exhibition, for in many ways these images are more challenging. In the photograph of the twelve-year-old girl in the 2008 exhibition there are no squalid surroundings, but simply the girl standing facing forwards in a kind of half-light with no surrounding features visible. Here the concern seems to have been with the very idea of nudity with such a young model.

11. An artist may, of course, not have it in mind to convey anything at all – any insight, say, into human life – but merely to produce a kind of aesthetic pleasure.

12. Note that while voyeurism is generally thought to involve watching others secretly for sexual pleasure, the pleasure of watching derived by the voyeur need not be sexual. (Note the distinction here between common usage and the clinical psychological condition.)

13. Surely a much more plausible example of the sexualization of adolescents is the display of very young adolescents in some fashion photographs. While many people have moral reservations about such photography, this practice has not attracted the kind of extreme moral outrage that was directed at Henson's photographs of young people. While I do not want to push the point, my suggestion that Henson's images truthfully represent the sexuality of his young models perhaps provides some explanation of why that might be.

14. To consider a different point, it may be that a work of art is corrupt yet not corrupting. Indeed, it may be that a work of art that we recognize as corrupt can be morally edifying in virtue of that very act of recognition. As Robert Stecker says on this point, "the expression in a work of attitudes ranging from the morally uncertain to the reprehensible may do some good. For example, the latter may inadvertently harden us against behaviour based on such an attitude" (2005: 210).

15. I am *not* saying that either you accept that Henson's work is morally unobjectionable or you are guilty of moralism. The fact that someone has moral

qualms about Henson's work does not itself make them a moralizer; as I have already said in Chapter 1, if someone does not see themselves as fitting my description of a moralizer then so be it. Indeed, I would myself be guilty of something akin to moralism if I were to resort to this kind of crude moral accusation. I *am* saying, however, that morality requires reflection on one's own moral judgements and the motivations for them, and that the moralizer is peculiarly averse to that. So if a person is hostile to the mere invitation to think again about Henson and what we might make of his work, I suppose they are *ipso facto* guilty of moralism on my account.

16. This chapter has the limited aim of examining moralism about art, and I make no claims about the justification for censorship of obscene material. Similarly, I offer no suggestions as to what steps might be taken to protect children from real exploitation by artists. On the second point, I note that the Australian government is currently considering possible guidelines for artists in using underage models.

17. Many entirely innocent contexts are, for some people, opportunities for such pleasure. For Humbert Humbert, Lolita's tennis matches were just such an opportunity.

18. My point here is reminiscent of Hart's point against Devlin in their debate over legal moralism. Devlin there argues that if the reasonable man, the man in the street, has a "real feeling of reprobation" (quoted in Hart [1959] 1993: 280) with respect to some practice, then society has the right to use the sanctions of the criminal law to eradicate that practice. Hart replies: "In his reaction against a rationalist morality and his stress on feeling, he has I think thrown the baby out with the bath water ... When Sir Patrick's lecture was first delivered *The Times* greeted it with these words: 'There is a moving and welcome humility in the conception that society should not be asked to give its reason for refusing to tolerate what in its heart it feels intolerable.' This drew from a correspondent in Cambridge the retort: 'I am afraid that we are less humble than we used to be. We once burnt old women because, without giving reasons, we felt in our hearts that witchcraft was intolerable.' ... We are not, I suppose, likely, in England, to take again to the burning of old women for witchcraft or to punishing people for associating with those of a different race or colour, or to punishing people again for adultery. Yet if these things were viewed with intolerance, indignation, and disgust, as the second of them still is in some countries, it seems that on Sir Patrick's principles no rational criticism could be opposed to the claim that they should be punished by law. [But] ... why should we not summon all the resources of our reason, sympathetic understanding, as well as critical intelligence, and insist that before general moral feeling is turned into criminal law it is submitted to scrutiny of a different kind from Sir Patrick's?" (*ibid.*: 282).

## 4. Overweening morality

1. See in particular Williams's *Ethics and the Limits of Philosophy* (1985).

2. There are other ways that we might frame the charge that morality may overween in our lives that do not trace this to the demands of certain moral theories, and specifically to the contemporary versions of utilitarianism and Kantianism that are Williams's target. For example, in her seminal paper "Moral Saints", Susan Wolf suggests that a person "whose every action is as morally good as possible, a person, that is, who is as morally worthy as can be ... does not constitute a model of personal well-being toward which it would be particularly rational or good or desirable for human beings to strive" (1982: 419). Yet while she discusses the ways in which a person's adherence to Kantian or utilitarian principles might lead to such a life, she claims she is not "really criticizing either Kantianism or utilitarianism" (*ibid*: 435). Rather, her point seems to be that in deciding how to live we need to consider a point of view outside the moral point of view, the point of view she calls "the *point of view of individual perfection*" (*ibid*: 437). This point of view, she suggests, "provides us with reasons that are independent of moral reasons for wanting ourselves and others to develop our characters and live our lives in certain ways" (*ibid*). In many ways I am sympathetic to Wolf's argument. However, as I will argue, I do not think that the committed utilitarian or Kantian can so easily insulate themselves from what I think is a tendency internal to such theories to overween in our lives. Indeed, Wolf has herself suggested in a more recent paper that we abandon the whole idea of a moral point of view such as these theories propose (Wolf 1999).

3. In a footnote to his "Consequentialism, Integrity and Demandingness" (2009: 146 n.8), Alan Thomas also suggests that Cullity's approach to the problem of moral demandingness is susceptible to Williams's "one thought too many" objection, although Thomas does not expand on this claim in this paper.

4. Note that the problem, as I shall understand it, with talking about what is morally permitted is not simply, as Cullity says, that it suggests "a narrow-mindedly legalistic approach to ethical thought" (Cullity 2004: 15). My concern is with the proper scope and limits of moral thought or reflection in our lives. And the charge that certain conceptions of morality, including Cullity's, are potentially overweening cannot be addressed simply by suggesting, as Cullity does, that "everything I say could be rephrased instead as a discussion of the ways of living that could deserve our respect or emulation, all things considered" (*ibid*.). A conception of human life such as the one Williams offers based on some idea of character broadly construed – which offers an adequate response to morality's overweening in our lives – *is* worthy of our respect or emulation, but there is no way of rephrasing Cullity's argument consistent with that conception of human life.

5. So the argument against impartiality is not the objection suggested by, for example, Robert Louden about whether we can "act consistently on our deep

concern with the good of our friends for their own sake if morality obligates us to give 'equal time' to the legitimate moral claims of all, including total strangers" (1992: 23–4).

6. There are some demands that friends obviously cannot make on each other. I cannot out of friendship demand that my friend harm another innocent person. The point is not just that it would be morally wrong to act like this; it is that such demands are no part of the demands of friendship as we understand it.

7. I say that this response to the problem of Extreme Demand leads to talking about our personal relationships and projects as permissions because, once the Extreme Demand is rejected on Cullity's appropriately impartial point of view, the question remains as to what is the extent of the demands placed on us by the world poor, and for Cullity, and those who argue in a similar way, the impartial point of view from which the Extreme Demand is rejected is supposed to answer a question of that form.

8. Note that this is not to say that every choice is a moral one but merely to point out that there is no human action outside the scope of morality's purview.

9. Note that the issue here is not that impartial morality has some kind of *priority*. For of course the impartialist may concede that in some contexts personal relationships and projects may take priority. The issue is rather that it is from the impartial point of view that we are to determine when personal relationships and projects *may* take priority. My objection is not that morality will always take priority but that morality gets to decide when and if something else may take priority to some extent over it.

10. What will perhaps be clearer now is why the objections I have raised to contemporary versions of utilitarianism and Kantianism cannot be met simply by positing as Wolf does (see note 2, above) the point of view of individual perfection as distinct from the moral point of view. Wolf, I think, really concedes too much – actually, the crucial point – to such theories when she says it "may not be the case that the perfectionist point of view is like the moral point of view in being a point of view we are ever *obliged* to take up and express in our actions" (1982: 437). For once we have granted to such theories the special notion of obligation that Wolf alludes to here, where there is a conflict between the reasons provided by the moral point of view and reasons provided by the point of view of individual perfection, we are obliged to resolve that conflict in accordance with the impartial demands of these theories. So the reasons derived for the perfectionist point of view, if they survive, will appear once again as, for example, permissions.

11. Of course there may be *some* context in which the question of whether it is permissible to spend time with a friend might reasonably come up. For example, one might ask whether it is permissible, or simply right, to keep drinking with a friend in my back garden rather than help save my neighbour's house from burning down. More generally, it is always possible to "stack the deck"

in favour of impartial morality simply by thinking up some scenario in which it is obvious to anyone that a question about whether some act is permissible or simply morally right should come up. But even in such cases it need not be impartial moral consciousness that motivates our thoughts about what is decisive in answering that question. It may be, thinking of my example above, that to keep on drinking and making merry with my friend strikes me as indicating a want of fellow feeling or sympathy (which I shall discuss briefly later) and wrong for that reason. There is no parity between the claim that there is always some context in which a question might arise about the moral rightness of pursuing some personal relationship or project (which any conception of ethics might hold) and the claim that what should *morally* motivate me here is the deliverances of some impartial moral consciousness.

12. Terry Jones, the director of *The Meaning of Life*, has not had much luck with the Irish Film Censorship Board; his previous film with the Python team, *The Life of Brian*, was also banned in Ireland, as was the sex comedy *Personal Services*, which he also directed. Jones has joked that to his knowledge the Irish Film Censorship board has banned four films, three of which are directed by him.

13. So a particular religious based ethics, perhaps of an uncompromising puritanical variety, would also be overweening in much the same way.

14. It may be said that satire often itself serves to make a moral point or lesson. This is certainly true, for example, of Swift's *A Modest Proposal*. However, the kind of parody or mocking that occurs in satire need not have any lofty moral aims. It would stretch credulity to say that there was some overarching moral point to Rabelais's satire *Gargantua and Pantagruel*, for instance.

15. So, for example, Lamarque notes critic Anthony Lane's comment that "[n]ow, at a distance, the book reads better than it did; it feels lit with a kind of cold hellfire, and Ellis has become our most assiduous tour guide … to the netherworld of the nineteen-eighties" (quoted in Lamarque 2009: 290).

16. Williams acknowledges this challenge explicitly in *Ethics and the Limits of Philosophy* (1985).

17. In discussions of the moral demands placed on us by the world's desperately poor it is common to hold that immediacy is irrelevant to one primary moral reason to help others in need. So, for example, Peter Singer (1972) has introduced what has come to be called the lifesaving analogy. Roughly the argument here is that immediacy (to me) is not relevant to my obligation to aid those in life-threatening situations. Hence if I accept that I have an obligation to help a child drowning in a pond right in front of me if I could easily do so, then I should accept – so the argument goes – that I should give financial aid to those suffering in desperate poverty far away, again granted that I might easily do so (say, by phoning Oxfam with my credit card details). In my argument in this section I take issue with the assumption that immediacy to me is not – in the sense intended – relevant to my obligation to provide another with aid.

18. Wolf (1982) argues from somewhat similar concerns that the problem is not with utilitarian or Kantian theories but with the idea (in her view not essential to such theories) that we should be as morally good as we can be.

## 5. Moral judgement and moral reflection

1. I shall refer specifically to Diamond in this chapter.
2. The terminology of "thick" and "thin" derives originally from Bernard Williams. See his *Ethics and the Limits of Philosophy* (1985).
3. This is not to suggest that students should not be challenged, even challenged in ways they might find very disturbing, but to point to the limits to such challenge and to suggest that those limits cannot be spelled out in terms of moral concepts and fixed principles that are then just applied to the situation at hand.
4. For another interesting account of the ways in which such capacities of response may be involved in our moral life and agency, see Morton (2006).
5. To say that these responses are primitive is not to say that they are mere reflex reactions. While they are not mediated by particular thoughts, they nevertheless bear the mark of intentionality, of mind. So we might say that the responses themselves involve thought that they are continuous with, to use Crary's terms, "an episode of thought".
6. I shall consider particular examples, including from social psychology, later in this chapter.
7. It is important to stress that the kind of illumination at issue here is not restricted to what may be termed intellectual pursuits. Consider, for example, what a simple act of kindness either witnessed or received may reveal to us about the value of a human life. In this connection Iris Murdoch, after asking "What is a Good man like?", goes on to suggest that it "is perhaps most convincingly met with in simple people – inarticulate, unselfish mothers of large families" ([1970] 1985: 53). I thank Steven Tudor for reminding me of this example.
8. I find this explanation for Jim jumping quite implausible. At the time the other four white crew members had in fact given up on Jim, even called him a coward, for refusing to help them release the lifeboat. So when the three men in the lifeboat call back to the ship, it is for *George* – the third engineer (who unbeknown to them has died of a heart attack on deck) – to jump, not *Jim*. If Jim had been motivated by a concern for how he would appear to these men, he may have helped them but on that account he certainly would not have jumped into their lifeboat after refusing to help them. While Jim has contempt for the other white crew members they likewise have contempt for him, as becomes apparent when they discover in the darkness that it is Jim who has jumped, not George. The most obvious explanation for Jim jumping here, and it says nothing very special about him, is fear for his own life.

9. In a similar vein, Joanne Wood suggests that "[i]n accepting the consequences without acknowledging any guilt, Jim remains a Kantian hero to the end" (1987: 69).

10. The tendency to try to resolve the ambiguities over Jim's final act is not restricted to philosophical commentaries. A host of influential literary readings over the years have also attempted to explain Jim's actions in terms of defining character traits. So Albert Guerard suggests that "Marlow realizes [Jim] has not escaped the egoism and pride which menaced him from the start" (1965: 144); similarly Tony Tanner suggests that Jim is "egoistic to the end" (1963: 55); while Ian Watt suggests more positively that Jim passes the test he failed on the *Patna* in not running away from his fate in Patusan and that he "dies for honour" (1980: 356). Somewhat more in line with my own reading, Jacques Berthoud suggests that "[i]t seems to me a measure of Conrad's humanity that he does not close his novel on a note of unqualified heroic absolutism. … Whatever his death may mean to Jim, for Marlow it does not resolve, but crowns, the ambiguity of a tormented career" (1978: 92–3).

11. A detailed discussion of the relevant literature is beyond the scope of this book. But for further discussion of *Lord Jim* in relation to the influence of character, see Goldie (2004: chs 3, 4) and Doris (1998; 2002: ch. 8). Of particular bearing for my discussion of *Lord Jim* is Peter Goldie's suggestion that "we should be *circumspect about our own motives and character traits*" (Goldie 2004: 98).

12. This particular experiment involved a group of seminarians at Princeton, some of whom were asked to prepare a talk on the parable of the Good Samaritan while others were asked to prepare a talk on the job prospects for seminarians. The set-up of the experiment involved telling some of each group that they had plenty of time to get to the venue for the talk, others that they had just enough time and others that they would need to rush. On the way to the venue it was further arranged that the seminarians should pass an apparently distressed colleague. As reported by Goldie, "Of those with plenty of time 63 per cent helped, of those with enough time 45 per cent helped, and of those in a hurry only 10 per cent helped" (2004: 62–3). For a more extended discussion of the empirical research in this area, see Doris (1998, 2002).

13. It is not clear, for example, whether the empirical research cited by Doris among others motivates the kind of radical scepticism about character that he appears to be arguing for (Doris 1998, 2002). One might think that having a properly developed character is rare so that it would not show up in the aggregate data from these kinds of social experiments. For a critical appraisal of Doris (1998), see Sreenivasan (2002). Related to this, it is interesting that Doris himself, in discussing *Lord Jim*, suggests that "Jim's ruin was not his failure on the *Patna*, but the adolescent understanding of heroism that dictated his response to that failure" (2002: 162). This explanation depends on the idea that Jim, although now a grown man, has not, as we might say, entirely grown

up: that is, I would suggest, on the idea that Jim's character has not properly formed in one important respect.

14. It is worth noting that the specific contribution a novel like *Lord Jim* might make to our understanding is a clearer sense of *what it is* that we need to entertain about ourselves, and that is not something we might achieve simply by reading the empirical studies I referred to earlier.

15. This is not to deny then, as Rupert Read has pointed out to me, that the French lieutenant at least shudders at the thought of Jim's lost honour.

16. Discussions of *Lord Jim*, both philosophical and sometimes literary, have tended to ignore the significance of the French lieutenant's perspective on Jim, which is not to say that my positive appraisal of the lieutenant is completely idiosyncratic. So, Suresh Raval suggests, in a similar vein, that the lieutenant's remarks that I have just quoted illustrate that he "represents the authority of practical reason and experience, an authority that derives its power, not from an unqualified assertion of the self, but from a recognition of the self's liabilities" (1981: 392).

17. And of course many readers, for example Eldridge (1989) and Wood (1987), do not find fault here.

## 6. Moral difference

1. I do not want to suggest that self-scrutiny will always involve reflecting on one's character. Of course sometimes we need to reflect simply on what our desires or values are in order to get clearer about what really matters to us. Also, we might need to reflect on the meaning of those moral ideas, principles or concepts that we endorse, and this too perhaps can be a kind of self-scrutiny. I thank Oskari Kuusela for drawing these further possibilities of self-scrutiny to my attention.

2. Of course there are uncontroversial ways in which different people might reach different moral judgements in the same situation and both be correct. The most obvious of those perhaps relate to different roles people might occupy that are relevant to their judgement, which is just to say really that different people may not be in the same situation: the situation of a fireman contemplating whether to enter a burning building to save those trapped inside is not the same situation as a member of the general public in the same place. Less obviously, some non-moral features of my character in the broadest sense will also be relevant to my judgement for much the same kind of reason. Two members of the general public contemplating whether to enter the burning building mentioned above might properly reach different judgements about whether or not they ought to enter the building depending on whether one of them, say, has a heart condition or is prone to suffering panic attacks. But again this is just to concede that two agents are not in the same situation.

Certain infirmities, including of character, are part of what a particular agent has to deliberate *from* in deciding how they ought to act, since any agent's decision needs to be informed by their thinking about whether or not they, being the kind or person they are, can follow some course of action through to its successful completion.

3. Of course, as I have already noted, and more generally, the mere fact that an agent *claims* they morally cannot act in some way does not entail that their judgement is above criticism. Despite what an agent claims, we might think all the same, as Winch notes, that they made the wrong moral judgement. Three circumstances that Winch suggests may properly lead us to reject an agent's judgement are: (i) where it is clear to us that the agent has not after all considered the moral issues in making their judgement; (ii) where an agent's conception of right and wrong are profoundly different from our own; and (iii) where it is clear to us that the agent's claim is insincere. Winch's argument, however, concerns what we are to make of, and how we are to respond to, an agent's moral judgement where it does not suffer from these or any other related defect (see Winch 1972: 166).

4. Note that my own view of moral incapacity (Taylor 1995, 2001) differs markedly from that of Williams.

5. Of course it may be that someone wants to make a more general judgement that, in the face of world poverty, everyone in the West ought to change the way we live to some extent. The point is just that it does not follow from the fact that an agent claims they cannot live as others in the West do that they must *necessarily* make the more general judgement above.

6. For further readings of the ethical interest for moral philosophy in *Disgrace*, see Attridge (2004) and Crary (2010).

7. David Wiggins argues that Winch has failed to attend to Melville's "thought that war makes men like Captain Vere selectively but dangerously mad" (1987: 172).

8. See in particular Coetzee's 1997/8 Tanner Lectures, *The Lives of Animals* (1999) and his subsequent novel based in part on these lectures, *Elizabeth Costello* (2004).

9. Here it is important to note that, according to Louden, "the doctrine of moral self-perfection, properly understood, is quite distinct from ... 'self-centred' views about human motivation" (1992: 16).

10. I am not saying that the situations here are strictly moral dilemmas in the technical sense that is used in moral philosophy. In that sense a moral dilemma is a situation in which whatever an agent does will be wrong, such that there is no morally right way for them to act. For clearly, as I have explained, Winch thinks there is a morally right way for him to act in Vere's situation; only he thinks it is right *for him*, and not universally so.

11. This is not to say that defenders of the universalizability thesis will necessarily deny the existence of irresolvable moral conflict in some sense. Louden,

for instance, acknowledges such conflict. However, those committed to the universalizability thesis will reject the kinds of personal moral modalities suggested here in response to such conflicts. So, for example, we can see the continued hold of the universalizabilty thesis in the following remarks from Louden. Considering the role of conflict-recognizing moral theories, he suggests: "we ourselves should be able to make more informed decisions by considering *how other people faced with similar dilemmas arrived at their own decisions*, as well as by learning from the consequences of such decisions" (Louden 1992: 132, emphasis added). I would not deny that there is a place for such consideration, but beyond this, I have argued, an agent may need to consider what is morally possible *for them*.

## 7. Public moralism

1. Coady classifies moralism into six basic types: "moralism of scope, moralism of unbalanced focus, moralism of imposition or interference, moralism of abstraction, absolutist moralism, and moralism of deluded power" (2008: 17). Of particular relevance to realist criticisms of morality, and a relative focus for Coady, is morality of scope. Here realist criticism amounts to questioning what Coady calls the "dominance" of morality; that is, "its trumping all other considerations whenever it is relevant to them", as well as morality's "comprehensiveness", that is, "its being universally relevant whether it trumps other considerations or not" (*ibid.*: 19). In this chapter I shall largely be concerned with morality of scope in this sense.

2. For an extended examination of the challenges faced by liberal democracies in dealing with the threat of terrorist attack, see Ignatieff (2004).

3. The concept of extreme emergency comes from Michael Walzer and is used by him to describe the kind of situation Britain faced against Germany in the Second World War. In particular he uses it to defend the "terror bombing" of German cities during the early part of the war. The bombings were justified, Walzer suggests, because Britain faced "an ultimate threat to everything decent in our lives, an ideology and a practice of domination so murderous, so degrading even to those who might survive, that the consequences of its final victory were literally beyond calculation, immeasurably awful" (2000: 253).

4. Of course dirty-hands-type situations are not restricted to political action (I shall consider a similar conflict in relation to professional roles later in this chapter). However, such situations are a much more common feature for those who occupy high office and exercise the kind of power over people and events that such office involves, indeed requires.

5. This is by no means an abstruse philosopher's example. Consider for example the continuing tension on the Korean peninsula caused by the actions of North Korea.

6. So it seems implausible to claim that Wall's point was simply that Britain's involvement in what was essentially a civil war would be morally wrong. For, as I shall argue below, a political leader's decision in such a case will depend crucially on other considerations. Thus a further question for a foreign secretary in such a case will be: what are our interests in the region and what are the implications for them in intervening?

7. For a discussion of this and other moral conflicts related to the role of a defence lawyer, see, for example, Freedman (1966).

8. The relationship between morality and politics is the subject of much philosophical debate. For example, some philosophers have held that the obligations of public life, including the obligations of high political office, can in fact be derived from ordinary morality. However, another possibility advanced by Thomas Nagel (1978) is that, while what we may now call public morality is not directly derivable from ordinary morality, public and ordinary morality are each derivable from a common source.

9. I do not mean to suggest here that political leaders have a mandate to use violence, or necessarily any mandate at all, to ensure that their state continues *in its present form*. Indeed, the ability to initiate radical reform in the interests of the long-term viability of the state is an important aspect of the role of political leaders. F. W. de Klerk's role in ending apartheid in South Africa would seem to be an example here. I thank Rupert Read for helping me to clarify this point.

10. This pamphlet was written by Anscombe in 1956 in opposition to the University of Oxford awarding an honorary degree to President Truman.

11. It might be objected that my SUV driver may have been willing to be part of collective action for change yet reasonably felt under no obligation to take individual action. Here I make three points: first, collective action for political change starts with commitments and sacrifices by individuals; second, giving up what I suggested was essentially a symbol of lifestyle (maybe buying a smaller, more fuel-efficient car) was hardly a big sacrifice given the kind of injustice the driver seemed to be protesting against; third, given that this was a brand new vehicle and the West's supposedly morally problematic dependence on oil from the Gulf was not new, I have my doubts about the driver's enthusiasm for the kind of change he was advocating.

12. I cannot attempt here to specify in detail the full range of such qualifications. Let me say only that such qualifications would of course involve certain basic moral principles or ideas along with various practical or institutional limitations as I have briefly alluded to above.

13. One could argue of course that certain ideals are realizable. In the case of aesthetic ideals that notion strikes me as more depressing than hopeful. What could we look forward to from art in such a case? More of the same? In the case of a moral and/or political ideal, such as the ideal of justice, we might have different intuitions. Yet even here, and given the changing nature of human

social interactions, there may perhaps always be scope for striving towards the ideals of justice in constantly changing social circumstances.

14. I should note that Pearson's criticisms here, and his own suggestions about how the problems of Indigenous communities may be solved, are contested within Indigenous communities. What such communities would not contest though, I think, is the failure of Indigenous policy over many years to improve the plight of Indigenous Australians. All I am suggesting here is one reason for that failure.

15. I acknowledge that this is not the only ideal in play here. A further aim of such centres is, I think, simply to provide Indigenous Australians with a comfortable and safe study space in what is for many an alien environment.

# Bibliography

Alweiss, L. 2003. "On Moral Dilemmas: Winch, Kant and Billy Budd". *Philosophy* **78**(2): 205–18.

Anscombe, G. E. M. 1981. "Mr Truman's Degree". In *The Collected Philosophical Papers of G. E. M. Anscombe*, vol. 3, *Ethics, Religion and Politics*, 62–71. Oxford: Blackwell.

Armstrong, J. 2008. "In Liberal Democracy, Ideals Inspire". *The Australian* (10 October): 14. www.theaustralian.com.au/news/arts/in-a-liberal-democracy-ideals-inspire/story-e6frg8q6-1111117709824 (accessed October 2011).

Attridge, D. 1981. "The Language of Poetry: Materiality and Meaning". *Essays in Criticism* **31**(3): 228–45.

Attridge, D. 2004. "Age of Bronze, State of Grace: *Disgrace*". In his *J. M. Coetzee & the Ethics of Reading: Literature in the Event*, 162–91. Chicago IL: University of Chicago Press.

Atwell, J. 1976. "A Note on Decisions, Judgments, and Universalizability". *Ethics* **77**(2): 130–34.

Berthoud, J. 1978. *Joseph Conrad: The Major Phase*. Cambridge: Cambridge University Press.

Best, H. D. 1829. *Personal and Literary Memorials*. London: Henry Colburn.

Brudney, D. 1998. "*Lord Jim* and Moral Judgment: Literature and Moral Philosophy". *Journal of Aesthetics and Art Criticism* **56**(3): 265–81.

Carroll, N. 1996. "Moderate Moralism". *British Journal of Aesthetics* **36**(3): 223–38.

Carroll, N. 1998. "Moderate Moralism versus Moderate Autonomism". *British Journal of Aesthetics* **38**(4): 419–24.

Cavell, S. 1979. *The Claim of Reason*. Oxford: Oxford University Press.

Coady, C. A. J. (ed.) 2006. *What's Wrong with Moralism?* Oxford: Blackwell.

Coady, C. A. J. 2008. *Messy Morality: The Challenge of Politics*. Oxford: Oxford University Press.

Coetzee, J. M. 1999. *The Lives of Animals*. Princeton NJ: Princeton University Press.

Coetzee, J. M. 2000. *Disgrace*. London: Vintage.

Coetzee, J. M. 2004. *Elizabeth Costello*. London: Vintage.

Coleman, P. 1974. *Obscenity, Blasphemy, Sedition: 100 Years of Censorship in Australia*. Sydney: Angus & Robertson.

Committee on Homosexual Offences and Prostitution 1957. *Report of the Committee on Homosexual Offences and Prostitution* (The Wolfenden Report). London: HMSO.

Conrad, J. [1900] 2007. *Lord Jim*, A. Simmons (ed.). London: Penguin.

Crary, A. 2007. *Beyond Moral Judgment*. Cambridge, MA: Harvard University Press.

Crary, A. 2010. "J. M. Coetzee, Ethical Thinker". In *J. M. Coetzee and Ethics*, A. Leist & P. Singer (eds), 249–68. New York: Columbia University Press.

Cullity, G. 2004. *The Moral Demands of Affluence*. Oxford: Oxford University Press.

Dancy, J. 1993. *Moral Reasons*. Oxford: Blackwell.

Devlin, P. 1965. *The Enforcement of Morals*. Oxford: Oxford University Press.

Diamond, C. 1991. "Anything but Argument?" In her *The Realistic Spirit*, 291–308. Cambridge, MA: MIT Press.

Diamond, C. 1997. "Moral Differences and Distances: Some Questions". In *Commonality and Particularity in Ethics*, L. Alanen, S. Heinämaa & T. Wallgren (eds), 197–234. Basingstoke: Palgrave Macmillan.

Doris, J. 1998. "Persons, Situations and Virtue Ethics". *Nous* **32**(4): 504–30.

Doris, J. 2002. *Lack of Character: Personality and Moral Behaviour*. Cambridge: Cambridge University Press.

Dostoyevsky, F. 2004. *The Idiot*, D. McDuff (trans.). London: Penguin. Originally published in Russian as Идиот [*Idiot*] (1868).

Driver, J. 2006. "Moralism". See Coady (2006), 37–52.

Eldridge, R. 1989. "The Achievement of Autonomy: Marlow's Talk in *Lord Jim*". In his *On Moral Personhood: Philosophy, Literature and Self-Understanding*, 68–103. Chicago, IL: University of Chicago Press.

Freedman, M. H. 1966. "Professional Responsibility of the Criminal Defense Lawyer: The Three Hardest Questions". *Michigan Law Review* **27**: 1469–84.

Fullinwider, R. K. 2006. "On Moralism". See Coady (2006), 5–20.

Gaita, R. 1991. *Good and Evil: An Absolute Conception*. Basingstoke: Macmillan.

Gaita, R. 1998. *A Common Humanity*. Melbourne: Text Publishing.

Gaut, B. 2007. *Art, Emotion and Ethics*. Oxford: Oxford University Press.

Goldie, P. 2004. *On Personality*. London: Routledge.

Guerard, A. 1965. *Conrad the Novelist*. Cambridge, MA: Harvard University Press.

Greer, G. 2008. "Through a Lens Darkly". *The Age* (2 June): 13. www.theage.com.au/opinion/through-a-lens-darkly-20080601-2kgo.html (accessed October 2011).

Hart, H. L. A. 1963. *Law, Liberty and Morality*. Oxford: Oxford University Press.

Hart, H. L. A. [1959] 1993. "Immorality and Treason". In *Legal Philosophy: Selected Readings*, T. C. Shiell (ed.), 279–83. Fort Worth TX: Harcourt Brace Jovanovich, 1993. Originally published in *The Listener* (30 July 1959).

Hawthorne, N. [1850] 1960. *The Scarlet Letter*. Cambridge MA: Riverside Press.

Heyward, M. 1993. *The Ern Malley Affair*. St Lucia: Queensland University Press.

Hill, G. B. (ed.) 1897. *Johnsonian Miscellanies*, vol. 2. London: Constable.

Ignatieff, M. 2004. *The Lesser Evil: Political Ethics in an Age of Terror*. Princeton, NJ: Princeton University Press.

Ingram, A. (ed.) 1986. *Joseph Conrad: Selected Literary Criticism and The Shadow-Line*. London: Methuen.

Isaksson, F. & L. Furhammar 1977. "The First Person Plural". In *Conflict and Control in the Cinema*, J. Tulloch (ed.), 384–95. Melbourne: Macmillan Australia.

Kagan, S. 1989. *The Limits of Morality*. Oxford: Clarendon Press.

Kolenda, K. 1975. "Moral Conflicts and Universalizability". *Philosophy* **50**(4): 460–68.

Lamarque, P. 2009. *The Philosophy of Literature*. Oxford: Blackwell.

Louden, R. 1992. *Morality and Moral Theory: A Reappraisal and Reaffirmation*. Oxford: Oxford University Press.

Marr, D. 2008. *The Henson Case*. Melbourne: Text Publishing.

Marr, D. & M. Wilkinson 2004. *Dark Victory*. Sydney: Allen & Unwin.

McDonald, J. 1988. "Gruesome Voyeurism or Social Comment?" *Sydney Morning Herald* (26 November): 91.

McDowell, J. 1978. "Are Moral Requirements Hypothetical Imperatives?" *Proceedings of the Aristotelian Society, supplementary vol.* **52**: 13–29.

McDowell, J. 1979. "Virtue and Reason". *Monist* **62**: 331–50.

McGrath, A. E. 1994. *Christian Theology: An Introduction*, 2nd edn. Oxford: Blackwell.

Melville, H. [1924] 1967. *Billy Budd*. In *Billy Budd and Other Stories*. Harmondsworth: Penguin.

Morton, A. 2006. "Moral Incompetence". In *Values and Virtues: Aristotelianism in Contemporary Ethics*, T. Chappell (ed.), 118–35. Oxford: Oxford University Press.

Murdoch, I. [1970] 1985. *The Sovereignty of Good*. London: Routledge & Kegan Paul.

Nabokov, V. [1955] 1995. *Lolita*. Harmondsworth: Penguin.

Nabokov, V. 1955. Conversation with Pierre Berton and Lionel Trilling, *Close-up*, CBC, 26 November 1955.

Nagel, T. 1978. "Ruthlessness in Public Life". In *Public and Private Morality*, S. Hampshire (ed.), 75–91. Cambridge: Cambridge University Press.

Nietzsche, F. [1878] 1996. *Human, All Too Human*, R. J Hollingdale (trans.). Cambridge: Cambridge University Press.

Nussbaum, M. 1990. *Love's Knowledge*. Oxford: Oxford University Press.

Nussbaum, M. 2003. "Tragedy and Justice: Bernard Williams Remembered". *Boston Review* 20(5). www.bostonreview.net/BR28.5/nussbaum.html (accessed October 2011).

O'Neill, O. 1980. "Review: *The Moral Status of Animals*, by Stephen Clark". *Journal of Philosophy* 77(7): 445.

Owen, D. 1995. *Balkan Odyssey*. London: Indigo Press.

Pearson, N. 2000. "The Light on the Hill". Ben Chifley Memorial Lecture, 2000. Transcript available at www.australianpolitics.com/news/2000/00-08-12a.shtml (accessed October 2011).

Raval, S. 1981. "Narrative and Authority in *Lord Jim*: Conrad's Art of Failure". *ELH: English Literary History* 48(2): 387–410.

Raz, J. 2003. "The Truth in Particularism". In *Moral Particularism*, B. Hooker & M. Little (eds), 48–78. Oxford: Oxford University Press.

Read. R. 2010. "Wittgenstein's *Philosophical Investigations* as a War Book". *New Literary History* 41(3): 593–612.

Scheffler, S. 1992. *Human Morality*. Oxford: Oxford University Press.

Singer, P. 1972. "Famine, Affluence and Morality". *Philosophy and Public Affairs* 1(1): 229–43.

Sreenivasan, G. 2002. "Errors about Error: Virtue Theory and Trait Attribution". *Mind* 111(1): 47–68.

Stecker, R. 2005. *Aesthetics and the Philosophy of Art*. Lanham, MD: Rowman & Littlefield.

Tanner, T. 1963. *Conrad: Lord Jim*. London: Edward Arnold.

Taylor, C. D. 1995. "Moral Incapacity". *Philosophy* 70(2): 273–85.

Taylor, C. D. 2001. "Moral Incapacity and Huckleberry Finn". *Ratio* 14(1): 56–67.

Taylor, C. D. 2002. *Sympathy: A Philosophical Analysis*. Basingstoke: Palgrave Macmillan.

Taylor, C. D. 2006. "Moralism and Morally Accountable Beings". See Coady (2006), 53–60.

Thomas, A. 2009. "Consequentialism, Integrity and Demandingness". In *The Problem of Moral Demandingness*, T. Chappell (ed.), 123–47. Basingstoke: Palgrave Macmillan.

Today 2008. *Today* television programme, Channel Nine Australia, 23 May.

Tovey, J., L. Kennedy & J. Dart 2008. "Art Obscenity Charges". *Sydney Morning Herald* (24 May): 1.

Tudor, S. 2000. *Compassion and Remorse: Acknowledging the Suffering Other*. Leuven: Peeters.

Unger, P. 1996. *Living High and Letting Die: Our Illusion of Innocence*. New York: Oxford University Press.

Walzer, M. 2000. *Just and Unjust Wars: A Moral Argument with Historical Illustrations*, 3rd edn. New York: Basic Books.

Watt, I. 1980. *Conrad in the Nineteenth Century*. London: Chatto & Windus.

Wiggins, D. 1987. "Truth, and Truth as Predicated of Moral Judgments". In his *Needs, Values, Truth*, 2nd edn, 139–84. Oxford: Blackwell.

Williams, B. 1981a. "Persons, Character and Morality". In his *Moral Luck: Philosophical Papers 1973–1980*, 1–19. Cambridge: Cambridge University Press.

Williams, B. 1981b. "Politics and Moral Character". In his *Moral Luck: Philosophical Papers 1973–1980*, 54–70. Cambridge: Cambridge University Press.

Williams, B. 1985. *Ethics and the Limits of Philosophy*. London: Fontana.

Williams, B. 1993. "Moral Incapacity". *Proceedings of the Aristotelian Society* **93**(1): 59–70.

Winch, P. 1972. "The Universalizability of Moral Judgments". In his *Ethics and Action*, 151–70. London: Routledge & Kegan Paul.

Winch, P. 1987. *Trying to Make Sense*. Oxford: Blackwell.

Wolf, S. 1982. "Moral Saints". *Journal of Philosophy* **79**(8): 419–39.

Wolf, S. 1999. "Morality and the View from Here". *Journal of Ethics* **3**: 203–23.

Wood, J. 1987. "*Lord Jim* and the Consequences of Kantian Autonomy". *Philosophy and Literature* **11**(1): 57–74.

Woollacott, M. 2005. "In Times of Crisis, the Media is the Moralist of the Story". *Sydney Morning Herald* (14 January): 17. www.smh.com.au/news/Opinion/In-times-of-crisis-the-media-is-the-moralist-of-the-story/2005/01/13/1105582654448.html (accessed October 2011).

# Index